RICH MAN,
POOR MAN

RICH MAN, POOR MAN

HERMAN P. MILLER

ILLUSTRATIONS BY BILL GORMAN

THOMAS Y. CROWELL COMPANY

ESTABLISHED 1834   NEW YORK

This book is dedicated to my parents,
whose love and understanding
made everything possible for me

INTRODUCTION *by* W. *Willard Wirtz*
SECRETARY OF LABOR

Statistics are at least as old as the Bible. The Old Testament's Book of Numbers recorded the first national census—the counting of the warriors of the tribes of Israel, all the men who were twenty years of age or older. The New Testament recounts the most famous census of all, Joseph and Mary going up to Bethlehem to record the payment of their taxes.

Down through history, the census taker was most often either a military recruiter or a tax collector. Tallying heads usually had a simple purpose, to facilitate the collection of men or money, until the Constitution of the United States enlarged the reasons for a government's wanting to know who lived within its boundaries. It provided for a census every ten years to apportion not only "direct taxes" but also seats in the House of Representatives.

Ever since the Founding Fathers introduced the idea of determining political representation according to government-gathered population statistics, the United States Government has been increasing the scope and uses of the numbers it garners. In 1790, the first census counted white males by age, and also white females, slaves, and free nonwhites. In 1850, census takers first inquired about the value of individual property holdings. In 1940, the first inquiries were made about personal income.

The government's economic statistics are now almost as commonplace a part of the news reports as government-issued weather statistics. Just as temperature, humidity, and wind velocity are compiled, analyzed, and reported, so too are wholesale and consumer prices, employment and unemployment figures, and various other indicators of the country's economic velocity.

For many of the nation's activities, both public and

private, it can be said, in the beginning is the number. Every morning, millions of newspaper readers are scanning statistical charts. Decisions affecting millions of men and billions of dollars are made on the basis of how certain numbers have fluctuated, whether they be such popularly followed indexes as the security and commodity markets or one of the innumerable indexes followed by specialists looking for clues that will enable them to chart the flow of merchandise and money across the country and between continents.

Nowadays, numbers often make as much news as names. The cost-of-living index determines changes in industrial wage rates. Percentages of economic growth are a subject of political debate. Gross national product, the balance of payments, housing starts—these are only a few of the numerous numbers that are the stuff of front-page news stories.

We are a number-minded people, measuring our bigness and even our badness (the *ten* most-wanted men) in terms of numbers. As Secretary of Labor, I am almost a statutory number-watcher. The two principal statistical agencies of the federal government are the Bureau of the Census, located within the Commerce Department, and the Bureau of Labor Statistics, an arm of the Labor Department. Both collaborate on one of the federal government's best-known statistical efforts—preparing the monthly statistics on employment and unemployment issued by the Department of Labor.

As with so many other specialized activities, the danger is always present that these numbers will become ends in themselves, rather than another means by which we seek to penetrate the meaning of what is happening in our complex society. Just as some baseball fans seem to become absorbed in batting averages to the exclusion of the batters, some economists and statisticians become more absorbed in their charts than in the lives that are being charted. An income distribution is, after all, the sum of the families who earn it. Behind the percentages are, always, people.

Rich Man, Poor Man is a splendid exposition of the human quantities that lie behind the numbers employed by the economic statistician. Dr. Miller's text demonstrates that the economic statistician can, by the way he uses his professional tools, be as useful an analyst of our social structure as the sociologist.

On the one hand, numbers can depersonalize, turning blood and sweat to dust. On the other, they can so summarize and concentrate facts that they become slogans and symbols. Who can forget the impact of F.D.R.'s reminder that "one-third of the nation" had failed to achieve a semblance of the American standard of living? In an earlier day, Jacob Riis awakened New York City's conscience by describing "how the other half lives."

Herman Miller's analysis of the lower economic strata of our "affluent society" is an antidote to self-satisfaction. He helps dispel the widespread notion that we have achieved a society in which all are well-off and some are merely better off. The poor, he proves, are still with us. Though they have become a smaller fraction of our population in recent decades, their number remains appallingly large.

Dr. Miller raises and discusses a number of questions that are enormously pertinent to the future well-being of the United States: How affluent, really, are most of us? How much richer are we likely to become in the next ten or twenty years? Who are the poor, how poor are they, and what is the contemporary meaning of poverty in the United States? Why are some prevented from sharing in America's growing abundance? What chance have those who have fallen behind of catching up? What policies should we pursue in order to make things better for more people?

Dr. Miller offers us the factual wherewithal for considering these questions. He also has useful suggestions as to their answers. These are contentious questions, of course, and well-intentioned men may differ as to the best answers. For the welfare of America, however, it is vital to consider them.

ACKNOWLEDGMENTS

This book is a by-product of seventeen years of work at the Bureau of the Census. Words are inadequate to express my gratitude to that wonderful organization for giving me the opportunity to develop and interpret income statistics.

Only those who know Sar Levitan can fully appreciate how lucky I am to count him as a friend and adviser. He was always there with a kind word and a way out of a difficult situation.

Many friends, teachers, and colleagues read the manuscript and made useful suggestions. I cannot list them all, but it would be gross negligence to omit Paul Boschan, Dorothy Brady, Gerhard Colm, Virginia Holran, Jay Gould, and Conrad Taeuber.

It has become customary to apologize to one's family for taking the time to write a book. I offer no such apology because this book was in many respects a family business. My children were active partners. June typed several drafts of the manuscript. She did a fine job for only twenty-five cents a page. Judi was an excellent proofreader. She got no pay since she was only serving an apprenticeship. My wife, Elaine, was a silent partner. She had the hardest job of all—listening to endless drafts. I'm sure it was only her interest in income that sustained her.

Contents

Tables

TABLES

What this book is about: Who gets what

For twenty-five years I have been trying to explain to people what an economic statistician does. Almost everyone is familiar with the work of doctors, dentists, lawyers, and accountants. In many circles, a mother referring to "my son, the doctor" immediately establishes her son—and herself—as a person to respect. But, what is there to say about "my son, the economic statistician"? Nothing, because most people don't even know what that is.

After years of patient discussion and education, I am beginning to make some headway. This progress has come generally from the subject matter of this book —income distribution.

Now, there is a term to contend with! Income distribution. It means different things to different people. You can tell from the sound of the words that it deals with who gets what. Using the universal language of poetry, Carl Sandburg sums up one of the central problems of income distribution in *The People, Yes*:

> "So, you want to divide all the money there is and give every man his share?"
> "That's it. Put it all in one big pile and split it even for everybody."
> "And the land, the gold, silver, oil, copper, you want that divided up?"
> "Sure—an even whack for all of us."
> "Do you mean that to go for horses and cows?"

"Sure—why not?"
"And how about pigs?"
"Oh to hell with you—you know I got a couple of pigs."

Poetry helps, but it has its limitations. Perhaps a simple illustration will help clarify the meaning of income distribution. Suppose for a moment that someone in your neighborhood went around and asked each family group how much money it made last year. Suppose further, just for the sake of argument, that each family told the truth. If you took these figures and arranged them in order from lowest to highest, you would have an income distribution. You would be able to say that so many families had less than $2,000 a year and so many had over $20,000 a year—that is, if there are any people this rich in your neighborhood. This kind of information is very useful. It could tell you what kind of a neighborhood you live in, which is not always easy to do just by looking at your neighbors or even by talking to them.

A recent example of the political significance associated with income distribution can be found in a *New York Times* editorial. This editorial cites a news report from Santiago, Chile, that troops fired on five thousand demonstrators, killing five and wounding scores. Explaining the cause of these riots, it quotes a pastoral issued by Chilean bishops: "Serious statistical studies, based on official sources, tell us that one-tenth of the Chilean population receives about half of the national income, while the remaining nine-tenths must subsist on the other half. This means that a great part of the working class does not receive wages commensurate with norms of social justice." Only a man close to sainthood, like the late Pope John XXIII, could be honestly thankful for his poverty. His emissaries in far-off Chile had a more realistic view of the importance most people attach to worldly goods and their distribution. At this point, of course, you have no way of knowing if the top income groups were getting a larger share in Chile than in other countries. That is one of the things you will discover in this book.

Figures on income distribution provide insight into many important social and economic problems. They show, for example, that the average Negro earns less than the average white, even when he has the same years of schooling and does the same kind of work. This is true not only in the South, but in the North as well.

Take another example. Is the income difference between the rich and the poor now less than it was twenty or thirty years ago? Most people think it is. What do the figures show? This is another problem that will be considered at some length and you will see that the answer is very complicated. It depends on how you define rich and poor; how you define income; what you do about taxes, undistributed profits, and capital gains; and how much value you place on intangibles such as better health, greater life expectancy, vacations with pay, and many other things. Although income figures have been collected in this country for more than thirty years, they are seldom presented in a way that is useful to the average citizen. Yet these facts are vitally important to everyone. They can refute misconceptions that have retarded the progress of our country. They provide the unarguable evidence on which public policy should rest. And they are a realistic guide to wise direction of personal affairs.

RICH MAN,
POOR MAN

CHAPTER I

Where do you fit in the income picture?

To start with, you must take my word for it that figures on income distribution are reasonably accurate. The next chapter will demonstrate why this faith is justified.

The American people received one-third of a trillion dollars in cash income in 1959. That is a lot of money: too much for anyone to imagine comfortably. But this vast sum had to be shared by fifty-eight million families and individuals. If each one got an equal share, it would only be $5,700. There is a number with some meaning! And to many it will seem surprisingly low.

There are many reasons why the average is low. For one thing, it assumes that each family gets exactly the same amount of money. That doesn't make much sense. Some families are larger than others; they "need" more. Some people work harder than others; they "deserve" more. Some people take bigger risks than others; they gain (or lose) accordingly. But there are also other reasons for the low average.

Below are figures showing the spread of income in the United States. They come from the last census. You may be interested in finding out where you fit in the income picture. Since only six different income groups are shown, these figures give an unrealistic view of the actual spread of incomes. It is really much greater than most people imagine. The noted economist Paul Samuel-

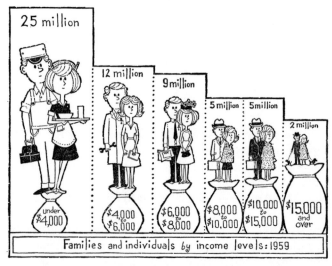

Table I-I. U.S. Bureau of the Census, *How Our Income Is Divided*, Graphic Pamphlet No. 2, 1963.

son has described income distribution in the following terms: "If we made an income pyramid out of a child's blocks, with each layer portraying $1,000 of income, the peak would be far higher than the Eiffel Tower, but almost all of us would be within a yard of the ground." This gives you some idea of the diversity that is compressed within these six income groupings.

The average factory worker earns about $100 a week, or more than $5,000 a year. In addition, many families have more than one worker. How then can there be 25 million families and individuals—nearly one-half of the total—with incomes under $4,000? There must be a joker somewhere.

Notice that unrelated individuals (a technical term for "one-person" families who live alone or as boarders in other people's homes) have been lumped with family groups consisting of two or more persons. That makes a big difference. One person living alone has only his own income and only himself to support. Where there are two or more people in a home, more than one can work —but there are also more mouths to feed.

It is obvious that before any more can be said about income, the unrelated individuals must first be separated from the families.

Unrelated individuals by income levels

At the time of the last census, there were 13 million unrelated individuals in the United States. They are often overlooked in the figures because their number is so small relative to the 165 million people who live in families. But they are a special group and they deserve special attention.

9% are under 25 ⎱	Young and old
34% are over 65 ⎰	
57% are 25–64	Working age

Together, the young and the old constitute more than two-fifths of all unrelated individuals. Many in the group called unrelated individuals are widows and widowers who spent most of their lives as family members. When their mates died, they kept their own homes and did not move in with children or enter old-age homes. Their incomes are low by all standards—half received less than $1,000 in the prosperous year of 1959. It was received largely as pensions and public assistance—although many of these people work.

3

Younger persons are also important in the unrelated individual population; they account for about one-tenth of the total. The average income of the youngsters was also low ($1,500), largely because their lack of skill and experience prevented them from commanding high wages.

Unrelated individuals in the most productive age brackets (twenty-five to sixty-four years) make up about three-fifths of the total. Their incomes are considerably higher than those cited for the younger and older persons; but they are nevertheless quite low by most standards. One-half had incomes under $2,500. The relatively low incomes of this group can be blamed on their inability to work, failure to find work, or their concentration in low-paying jobs when they are employed.

Families by income levels

The distribution of families by income levels is considerably different from that shown for unrelated individuals. At the time of the last census there were forty-five million families in the United States and they received nearly $300 billion. If this total had been equally divided, each would have received $6,600. In 1959, about six families out of every ten received less than that amount.

Millions of families in the United States still try to get by on less than $40 a week. There were six million such families, to be exact, in 1959. They represented 13 percent of all families but they received only 2 percent of the income. Many of them lived on farms where their cash incomes were supplemented by food and lodging that did not have to be purchased. Yet, even if this income were added to the total, it would not change the results very much.

At the golden apex of the income pyramid there were about one-half million families with incomes over $25,000. They represented 1 percent of the total but they received 8 percent of the income.

Table 1-2   *Families by income levels in 1959*

Income level	Number of families	Percent Families	Income
All families	45 million	100%	100%
Under $2,000	6 million	13	2
Between $2,000 and $4,000	8 million	18	8
Between $4,000 and $6,000	11 million	23	18
Between $6,000 and $8,000	9 million	19	20
Between $8,000 and $10,000	5 million	12	15
Between $10,000 and $15,000	5 million	11	19
Between $15,000 and $25,000	1½ million	3	10
$25,000 and over	½ million	1	8
Median income	$5,660		

U.S. Bureau of the Census, *How Our Income Is Divided,* Graphic Pamphlet No. 2, 1963.

Another way to view these figures is to examine the share of income received by each fifth of the families ranked from lowest to highest by income. In Table 1-3 you will see that in 1959 the poorest fifth of the families had incomes under $2,800; they received 5 percent of the total. In that same year, the highest fifth of the families had incomes over $9,000; they received 43 percent of the total.

Who sits at the top of the heap? The figures show that until you get to the very top the incomes are not so high. The top 5 percent of the families had incomes over $14,800. They received 18 percent of all the income. Families with incomes over $25,000 were in the top 1 percent and they received 8 percent of the total. Is $15,000 or $25,000 a year a very high income? To those near the base of the pyramid, it might be; but to a skilled worker with a working wife, an annual income of $15,000 may not seem like an unattainable goal. Economist Henry Wallich remarks that in America "the $25,000 family enjoys a variety of extras, but its basic form of living is not very obviously distinguishable from that of the $6,000 family."

If $25,000 a year is not a very high income, what is? Sociologist C. Wright Mills, in his book *The Power Elite*, defines the corporate rich as those with incomes of $100,000 a year or more. Relatively few American families have incomes this high. In 1959, there were only 28,000 individual income tax returns filed with adjusted gross incomes over $100,000. These returns accounted for about $5 billion or slightly more than 1 percent of the total distributed to the entire economy. These people certainly got more than their share; but the figures hardly support the view that the lower-income groups would be much better off if these very high incomes were confiscated and spread around more evenly. The fact of the matter is that they might be worse off if the golden goal of an income this high were removed.

The top income receivers are highly concentrated in the large metropolitan areas. The hundred largest urban centers contain about one-half of the population but about four-fifths of those who pay taxes on incomes over

$100,000. In 1959, the New York metropolitan area provided 6,700 tax returns reporting incomes over $100,000. Chicago and Los Angeles followed New York with about 1,800 high-income returns each.

Table 1-3   *Share of income received in 1959 by each fifth of U.S. families and by top 1% and 5%*

Families ranked from lowest to highest	Income range	Percent of income received
Lowest fifth	Less than $2,800	5%
Second fifth	Between $2,800 and $4,800	12
Middle fifth	Between $4,800 and $6,500	17
Fourth fifth	Between $6,500 and $9,000	23
Highest fifth	$9,000 and over	44
Top 5%	$14,800 and over	18
Top 1%	$25,000 and over	8

U.S. Bureau of the Census, *How Our Income Is Divided*, Graphic Pamphlet No. 2, 1963.

Are U.S. incomes too unequally distributed?

There is no objective answer to this question. It all depends on how unequally you think incomes should be distributed.

Around the turn of the century, the French poet and philosopher Charles Péguy wrote: "When all men are provided with the necessities, the real necessities, with bread and books, what do we care about the distribution of luxury?" This point of view went out of style with spats and high-button shoes. There is an intense interest in the distribution of luxury in the modern world.

Since we all cannot have as many material things as we should like, many people are of the opinion that those who are more productive should get more both as a reward for past performance and as an incentive to greater output in the future. This seems like a reasonable view, consistent with the realities of the world. Lincoln said: "That some should be rich shows that others may become rich and hence is just encouragement to industry and enterprise." The fact is that all modern industrial societies, whatever their political or social philosophies, have had to resort to some forms of incentives to get the most work out of their people.

Despite its reasonableness, this view has its critics. Some have argued that a man endowed with a good mind, drive, imagination, and creativity, and blessed with a wholesome environment in which these attributes could be nurtured, has already been amply rewarded. To give him material advantages over his less fortunate fellows would only aggravate the situation. The British historian R. H. Tawney wrote in his book *Equality:* ". . . some men are inferior to others in respect to their intellectual endowments. . . . It does not, however, follow from this fact that such individuals or classes should receive less consideration than others or should be treated as inferior in respect to such matters as legal status or health, or economic arrangements, which are within the control of the community."

Since there is no objective answer to the question as it has been formulated, it may be fruitful to set it aside and turn to the comparison of income in the United

States and other major countries for which such data are available.

Anyone who doubts that real incomes—purchasing power—are higher in the United States than in all other major countries just hasn't been around. But, how much higher? That is hard to say. How do you compare dollars, pounds, rubles, and francs? Official exchange rates are often very poor guides. Differences in prices, quality of goods, and living standards add to the complexity. In view of these problems, international comparisons are often made in terms of the purchasing power of wages. But even this measure has serious limitations. What constitutes a representative market basket in different countries, and how does one compare the market basket in one country with another? For example, Italians may like fish, which is relatively cheap, whereas Americans may prefer beef, which is quite expensive. How then would one compare the cost of a "typical" meal for families in the two countries? Because of this kind of problem, and many others, international comparisons of levels of living must be made with great caution. One study that casts some light on the subject was published in 1959 by the National Industrial Conference Board. It shows the amount of work it would take to buy the following meal for a family of four in several different countries. The items were selected from an annual survey of retail prices conducted by the International Labor Office:

Beef, sirloin	150 grams
Potatoes	150 grams
Cabbage	200 grams
Bread, white	50 grams
Butter	10 grams
Milk	.25 liter
Apples	150 grams

9

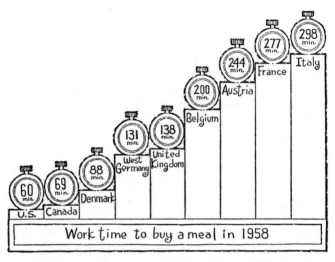

Work time to buy a meal in 1958

Table 1-4. Zoe Campbell, "Food Costs in Work Time Here and Abroad," *Conference Board Business Record*, December, 1959.

The results are shown in the pictograph (Table 1-4). The industrial worker in the United States had to work one hour to buy the meal above. The Canadian worker, whose level of living is not far behind that of his American cousin, had to work nine minutes more to buy the same meal. In Europe, the Danes came closest to the American standard, but even in Denmark the average worker had to toil one-half hour longer to feed his family. In West Germany and Great Britain it took more than two hours of work to buy the same meal and in Italy it took five hours. These and many other figures of a similar nature show that American workers are paid more in real terms than the workers of any other major country.

If international comparisons of levels of income are

difficult, comparisons of the distribution of income are virtually impossible. There are many opinions on the subject, but few of them are solidly based. Aldous Huxley, for example, believes that incomes are more unequally distributed in England than in France because "the highest government servants in England are paid forty or fifty times as much as the lowest." Following a similar line of reasoning, Max Eastman finds inequality greater in Russia than in the U.S. because the managing director of an American mining firm receives about forty times as much as one of his miners whereas a man in the same position in Russia may earn up to eighty times as much as a miner. This type of evidence might satisfy a literary man. The statistician is harder to please.

The United Nations, which has done some work in this field, cautions that "despite the intense interest in international comparisons of the degree of inequality in the distribution of income . . . surprisingly little incontrovertible evidence has been amassed. The margins of error of the available statistics . . . combined with differences in the underlying definitions . . . make it extremely hazardous to draw conclusions involving any but possibly a very few countries." No reputable scholar would deny the wisdom of these remarks. Yet judgments must be made and some figures, if they are carefully considered and properly qualified, are better than none. Even the world's leading authority on income distribution, Professor Simon Kuznets of Harvard University, agrees that international comparisons of income distribution, despite their serious limitations, have value because they are based on "a variety of data . . . rather than irresponsible notions stemming from preconceived and unchecked views on the subject."

Do the rich get a larger share of income in the United States than they do in other countries? According to the available evidence this is not the case. The United States has about the same income distribution as Denmark, Sweden, and Great Britain and a much more equal distribution than most of the other countries for which data are shown. There is no evidence that incomes are

Table 1-5   *Percent of income received by top 5% of families in selected countries*

United States	(1950)	20% *
Sweden	(1948)	20
Denmark	(1952)	20
Great Britain	(1951–52)	21
Barbados	(1951–52)	22
Puerto Rico	(1953)	23
India	(1955–56)	24
West Germany	(1950)	24
Italy	(1948)	24
Netherlands	(1950)	25
Ceylon	(1952–53)	31
Guatemala	(1947–48)	35
El Salvador	(1946)	36
Mexico	(1957)	37
Colombia	(1953)	42
Northern Rhodesia	(1946)	45
Kenya	(1949)	51
Southern Rhodesia	(1946)	65

* The numbers represent total income before taxes received by families or spending units.

Simon Kuznets, "Quantitative Aspects of the Economic Growth of Nations," *Economic Development and Cultural Change*, Vol. XI, No. 2, January, 1963, Table 3.

more widely distributed in any country than they are in the United States.

The figures in Table 1-5 classify the top 5 percent as "rich." This is a rather low point on the income scale. In the United States it would include all families receiving more than $15,000 a year. A more interesting comparison would be the share of income received by the top 1 percent ($25,000 or more per year) or perhaps even a higher income group. Such information, however, is not available for most other countries.

A comprehensive study of international comparisons of income was made in 1960 by Professor Irving Kravis of the University of Pennsylvania. He summarized the income distribution among the countries for which data are available in the following way:

> *More nearly equal distribution than U.S.*
> Denmark
> Netherlands
> Israel (Jewish population only)
> *About the same distribution as U.S.*
> Great Britain
> Japan
> Canada
> *More unequal distribution than U.S.*
> Italy
> Puerto Rico
> Ceylon
> El Salvador

CHAPTER II

Nearly everyone lies to the census man

At this point you probably want to know how much confidence you can place in these figures. A great deal. The income figures are surprisingly accurate and complete. The methods used to compile them are sound—the techniques have repeatedly demonstrated their worth for similar tasks. The results are double and triple checked—they match figures obtained from completely different, independent sources.

Most of the numbers quoted in this book were gathered by asking people to report how much money they make. Even though you know that the questionnaires used to collect these data were prepared, tested, and vouched for by the United States Bureau of the Census, you may still view the results with justified skepticism. Are the right people asked, in the right way? Do they really answer these kinds of questions, and, if so, do they tell the truth? Or was steelman Clarence Randall, in *The Folklore of Management*, correct when he judged that "the American people are getting annoyed at having their privacy invaded so incessantly by the little men and women who ask questions. At first they were intrigued and amused. Now they are bored and petulant. They solemnly give phony answers, and have a hearty laugh after they have closed the front door on the survey taker."

The first thing you must recognize is that the difficulty of collecting income data is highly exaggerated.

This is true despite the secrecy that generally surrounds private finances. Many persons who make party talk with intimate details of their sex habits are as reticent as Victorian ladies when it comes to the amounts of their paychecks—to their friends and neighbors, that is. To a professional interviewer who can guarantee the anonymity of their replies, they nearly always spill everything. Sex life, education, religion, family history, financial affairs—nothing seems too personal to be put into an anonymous statistical record. The census taker, backed by the prestigious power of the federal government and an unblemished record of secrecy spanning nearly two centuries, probably faces less resistance than other fact gatherers.

The great majority of people who are asked income questions in the census provide complete and accurate reports. (Each one seems to think that his neighbors are not so honest or so foolish.) Detailed records were kept in the 1960 census. They showed that 94 percent of the people who were asked the income questions answered them. The remaining 6 percent who did not answer were not all uncooperative. Some were temporarily away from home or they were in hospitals, jails, old-age homes, and similar places where the income information was not known by those who completed the census form for them. Some were home, but were sick and could not be interviewed. Others just did not know how much they made and refused to guess. On the basis of past experience, it seems unlikely that more than 1 percent refused to answer the income questions.

The most dramatic example of the kind of cooperation the Census Bureau gets from the American people is provided by a study that was made in the fall of 1960 to collect financial information from high-income families. In this study, six hundred families with incomes over

$15,000 were asked very detailed questions about their income, assets, financial transactions, and their attitudes toward various types of investments. Most interviews took two hours and more. No questions were spared. These interviews were conducted in four large metropolitan areas where people do not hesitate to say "no." Yet nearly 90 percent of the families provided complete information in all respects. Only 8 percent refused to be interviewed.

Today income information is regarded as one of the key facts collected in the census. Indeed, many people would not think of taking a census now without collecting information about income. But that was not the case twenty years ago.

"Wake up, America, before it is too late"

There is a long history of the collection of financial information in the population census. In 1850, census takers obtained information on the value of real estate owned by each individual. In 1860 and 1870 questions on bonds, stocks, mortgages, etc., were added. Yet, when it was proposed that information on personal income be collected for the first time in the 1940 census, the press and the Congress exploded. Newspaper editorials and cartoons lambasted the Census Bureau for asking such questions. The census taker was depicted as a sharp-nosed Uncle Sam called "Paul Pry." Senator Charles Tobey took to the airwaves with a nationwide address. "Wake up, America," he said, "before it is too late. Eternal vigilance is still the price of liberty. Stand up and fight. . . . These census questions demanding you to divulge your income manifestly violate your constitutional rights." He further attacked the questions as unwarranted prying which made available personal information to local people who were politically appointed as enumerators.

Fortunately, the income questions were not dropped in the 1940 census and a very useful body of information emerged. Very few people objected to the questions or refused to answer them, and so they were added again in th 1950 census. This time, Representative Clarence Brown of Ohio took up the cudgels. He charged the Truman Administration with "police state" methods in instructing census takers to ask individuals their income. He cited the inclusion of income questions in the census as "a perfect example of socialism in action. You have no right as an individual. You tell all to Washington. You knuckle under to the Government or go to jail."

It is surprising now how many people attacked the income questions in 1950. Arthur Krock of the *New York Times* wrote several learned pieces on the subject. George Sokolsky was vitriolic and misinformed. Even Herbert Hoover criticized the questions. Finally, the Congress Heights Citizens Association in Washington, D.C., after announcing that prizes of $10, $5, and $3 would be awarded for the best-decorated homes in its territory during Christmas, passed a resolution opposing the income questions in the 1950 census as "an infringement of the rights and freedom of citizens."

The income questions were asked in the 1950 census anyway, and the information was provided with very little objection. By 1960 there was no organized opposition to the inclusion of income questions in the census, and what has emerged is one of the most useful bodies of income statistics ever assembled.

But how good are the figures?

The decennial census of population in the United States is an actual nose count. An attempt is made to count every single human being in the country. In the 1940 census, every person in the country was asked to report wages and salaries (in addition to the other items included in the census). In 1950 the income survey was changed to a sampling basis. Every fifth person in the general census was questioned about his total income (not just wages and salaries). This technique was also followed in 1960, but the size of the sample was expanded to include every fourth family.

While everybody accepts 100 percent nose counts as accurate, many people are dubious about sample surveys. Their suspicion has been aroused—and rightly—by flagrant misuses of this method, particularly among advertisers.

It is easy to see, however, that samples can be useful —you don't have to drink the whole pot of soup to tell how it tastes; a couple of spoonfuls are enough. The technique gives honest, accurate results if two requirements are rigorously observed:

1. The soup must be well mixed. That is, the sample must be chosen so that it is faithfully representative of the whole and so that every person stands a known chance of being selected. Since the census asks income of every fourth family in every city, hamlet, and farm area in the entire country, this requirement is more than adequately fulfilled.

2. You must not taste the soup with a salt-laden spoon. That is, the test has to be fair. Questions must not be phrased in such a way that they will favor one kind of reply over another. The simplicity of

the census questions and the care taken in their composition eliminate this sort of bias.

Even with these precautions duly observed, one other fact about sample surveys should be faced. The answers they give must be considered not as absolutes, but in terms of a range. For example, the average (median) income of all families was given in Chapter I as $5,660. More properly this should be stated: the chances are two out of three that the average income that would be obtained in a complete census would differ from $5,660 by less than a dollar. This "statistical error" becomes more important when you try to slice up the raw data to draw conclusions about small groups. If you want to know the average income of professional men in the Chicago metropolitan area, you have to take an answer like this: the chances are two out of three that a complete census of professional men in Chicago would have produced a median that would differ from $7,385 by less than $40 (see Table A-1).

These qualifications are not serious. Even a 100 percent nose count is subject to errors (though of a different kind). The purely statistical errors in the census figures on income are small enough to be ignored. They are more than outweighed by other factors. The big question is: how can you tell if the answers that people give the census taker are correct? Maybe they lie. Maybe they just don't know.

The demonstration of truth

Income data are not like a crossword puzzle. You can't check them by looking up the answer in the next day's newspaper. What you can do is match one set of figures, obtained from one source, with related figures from other sources. The Census Bureau spent over a million dollars in 1950, and more than that in 1960, checking the accuracy of the census results.

The Office of Business Economics of the U.S. Department of Commerce provides one standard against which the census income figures can be checked. Each year this office prepares the figures on gross national product (the GNP that economists talk about). Compiled from such reliable data as the wage records of business firms and governmental agencies, they are regarded as among the most accurate of all figures prepared in Washington. The OBE estimated that the American people received $351,000,000,000 in cash income in 1959; the census measure of total income was $332,000,000,000, a difference of 6 percent (see Table A-2). The OBE figure is higher mainly because people forgot (accidentally? on purpose? who knows?) to tell the census man about much of their *extra* income beyond ordinary earnings. The figures on wages and salaries and self-employment income match almost exactly. If the 6 percent difference were applied to family income, the median would be raised to $6,000 (the census figure is $5,660).

A closer comparison can be made between the census and the Current Population Survey (CPS), which asks the income of a large nationwide sample every March. (See the Appendix for a detailed description of CPS.) In census years, many of the thirty-five thousand families covered in CPS are asked the same questions twice— once for CPS and once for the regular census. You may not be surprised to learn that a large proportion of them give different answers. But the differences tend to balance out, and the overall averages are remarkably similar (see Table II-1, pages 22–23).

A still closer check is provided by the Reinterview Surveys. The Census Bureau sends specially trained enumerators back to selected homes to ask the census questions—which had already been answered once—all over again. The main result of this test has been to turn up a large number of persons with very small incomes which they did not report the first time around. The probing of an expert interviewer often reveals some "forgotten" information.

It's dangerous to lie to the income tax man

The professional economist might be willing to accept the above comparisons as an assessment of census income statistics. The man in the street, however, is likely to be more hard-nosed. His idea of a valid check would be a comparison with income tax returns, much along the lines suggested by King Gama in Gilbert and Sullivan's *Princess Ida:*

> I know everybody's income and what everybody earns;
> And I carefully compare it with the income tax returns.

After all, tax returns are sworn statements. Some people may lie about their deductions; but the great majority report their income accurately, especially if taxes are withheld at the source. Why not compare a sample of census reports with income tax returns?

A very good idea, and that is exactly what is done. In 1950, income tax returns were located for a sample of five thousand families selected from the census, and the income information reported in both places was compared. The results of this study were published several years ago in a report prepared under the sponsorship of the National Bureau of Economic Research. They show that there is no significant difference overall between the incomes reported on tax returns and those reported in the census. Of course, not everybody reported the same income in both places. Far from it. In some cases the tax returns were higher and in others the census reports were higher. Overall, however, the differences balanced out

Table II-1	Comparison of income reported for 1959 and 1949 to Current Population Survey and Census by persons aged 14 and over

Sex, color, and residence	1959			1949		
	CPS	Census	Difference	CPS	Census	Difference
UNITED STATES		MALES				
Overall	$3,996	$4,103	$107	$2,346	$2,434	$ 88
White	4,208	4,319	111	2,471	2,573	102
Nonwhite	1,977	2,273	296	1,196	1,361	165
Nonfarm						
Overall	$4,230	$4,254	$ 24	$2,563	$2,613	$ 50
White	4,425	4,474	49	2,669	2,741	72
Nonwhite	2,347	2,409	62	1,476	1,571	95
Farm						
Overall	$1,696	$2,098	$402	$1,054	$1,339	$285
White	2,003	2,283	280	1,194	1,489	295
Nonwhite	664	778	114	488	577	89

Table II-I (*Cont.*)

Sex, color, and residence	1959			1949		
	CPS	Census	Difference	CPS	Census	Difference
UNITED STATES		FEMALES				
Overall	$1,222	$1,357	$135	$ 960	$1,029	$ 69
White	1,313	1,441	128	1,070	1,138	68
Nonwhite	809	909	100	495	590	95
Nonfarm						
Overall	$1,290	$1,397	$107	$1,049	$1,104	$ 55
White	1,361	1,478	117	1,158	1,200	42
Nonwhite	928	948	20	614	672	58
Farm						
Overall	$ 480	$ 731	$251	$ 392	$ 458	$ 66
White	665	826	161	433	533	100
Nonwhite	311	367	56	290	311	21

Data for 1959 from *U.S. Census of Population: 1960. General Social and Economic Characteristics, United States Summary,* Table 97; data for 1949 from *U.S. Census of Population: 1950, Characteristics of the Population, United States Summary,* Vol. II, Part I, Table 138; and CPS data from *Current Population Reports—Consumer Income,* Series P-60, Nos. 7 and 35, Tables 16 and 22 and underlying tabulations.

and the distribution was about the same. The discrepancy of $57 between the medians is not significant (see Table II-2).

Studies like those described above show that the income figures collected in the census cannot be far wrong. Still skeptical? You will find a more detailed and more technical evaluation of income statistics in the Appendix.

Table II-2   *Comparison of income
reported to 1950 Census
and Internal Revenue Service*

Family income	Percent reporting this income to census	Percent reporting this income on tax returns
No family income	1.5%	—
Loss rather than income	0.1	0.4%
$ 1 – $ 499	1.6	1.1
500 – 999	2.1	3.7
1,000 – 1,499	4.1	4.7
1,500 – 1,999	5.7	6.7
2,000 – 2,499	8.9	8.2
2,500 – 2,999	10.7	10.1
3,000 – 3,499	14.4	13.3
3,500 – 3,999	12.4	10.4
4,000 – 4,499	8.3	7.7
4,500 – 4,999	5.1	7.0
5,000 – 5,999	9.6	10.9
6,000 – 6,999	6.0	6.7
7,000 – 9,999	5.6	5.5
10,000 and over	3.8	3.7
Median income	$3,534	$3,591

Herman P. Miller and Leon R. Paley, "Income Reported in the 1950 Census and on Income Tax Returns," *Studies in Income and Wealth*, Vol. 23, Princeton University Press, 1958.

CHAPTER III

The pie gets bigger, the critics louder

Growth in average family income: 1929–62

What has happened to average family income since 1929? It is important to be very careful about dollars here because prices have risen and a dollar buys much less today than it did in 1929. Therefore, all figures will have to be expressed in dollars of constant purchasing power: 1962 dollars have been used for that purpose. Moreover, taxes have gone up as well as prices. In order to get a reasonable approximation of change in purchasing power the income should be measured after federal income taxes are deducted. The figures below satisfy both conditions.

There are some very important lessons to be learned from this set of numbers. In the first place, you can see that there is nothing magical about economic growth. Nothing is built into the economic system to guarantee that purchasing power—levels of living—will automatically go up each year. Indeed these few figures show that a decline began in 1929, lasted for about a decade, and was not fully recovered until World War II broke out.

During the war years there was, of course, a tremendous growth in real incomes. This resulted in a huge growth in savings, since there were few consumer goods around to be purchased. Factories were working at full steam and prices were controlled. As a result, real incomes rose by $800 in five years or about $160 per year.

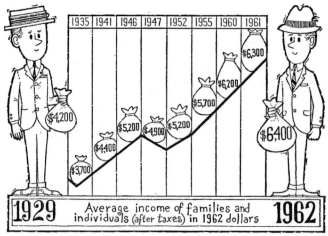

1935	1941	1946	1947	1952	1955	1960	1961

1929 — Average income of families and individuals (after taxes) in 1962 dollars — 1962

$3,700 $4,400 $5,200 $4,900 $5,200 $5,700 $6,200 $6,300

$4,200 $6,400

Table III-1. Jeanette M. Fitzwilliams, "Size Distribution of Income in 1962," *Survey of Current Business*, April, 1963, Table 1. Figures for 1935, 1941, and 1946 based on unpublished data.

The end of World War II did not bring the mass unemployment that so many economists had forecast, but the removal of price controls and the huge backlog of consumer demand backed by fat bank accounts forced prices up. Consequently there was a slight drop in purchasing power throughout most of the Truman Administration. Real family incomes were no higher in 1952, when Truman left office, than they were in 1945, when he entered it.

The Eisenhower Administration concentrated heavily on the control of inflation. The figures show that this policy was quite successful in terms of producing increases in family purchasing power. During the eight years of the Eisenhower Administration real family income rose by $1,000, or a little more than $100 a year.

This rate of growth has been continued in the Kennedy Administration.

The continuously high income levels of the past twenty years suggest that a new type of individual is now appearing on the American scene, one who has never had firsthand experience with severe economic depression. People born in 1942 are reaching maturity. Most of them have completed their education. Many are already married and having families. These youngsters have been reared in a period in which there has been no major economic depression. There have been recessions, to be sure; but these are minor economic ripples compared with the national depressions each previous generation of Americans experienced. Some of these young people live in depressed areas where jobs are scarce, and others have fathers who have been automated out of work. These are the exceptions rather than the rule. Never in the postwar era has the whole country suffered the bleak despair of the economic famines that came again and again, in 1837, 1857, 1893, 1907, 1921, and 1929.

Changes in the distribution by income levels: 1929–60

Averages can be very misleading. All that an average tells you is the amount that each one would get if the total were equally divided. The total is not equally divided and it makes a big difference just how unequally divided it is. A given level of income can provide palaces for live kings and pyramids for dead ones, but hovels and hunger for the mass of mankind; or it can be widely distributed and provide reasonably uniform levels of living for all. The levels may not be high, but they are often tolerable if the spread between the rich and the poor is not too great.

The figures for the United States show that the increase in the total and the average income since the depression of the thirties has been widespread throughout the population and has resulted in a general movement of families up the income scale. There have, of course, been many exceptions. The aged, uneducated, and unskilled have not moved ahead as fast as the others; but even for many of these groups the sharp edge of poverty has been blunted.

The more typical picture, particularly during the postwar years, has been one of gradually rising family incomes, due not only to the full-time employment of chief breadwinners, but also to the rising tendency for wives to supplement family income. These factors, in combination with the increasing productivity of American industry, have caused a persistent drop in the number and proportion of families at the lower income levels and a corresponding increase in the middle and upper income brackets. The extent of the increase in real family income can be seen most clearly in the table below. Here again, all the numbers are expressed in terms of constant purchasing power, so that the effects of inflation are eliminated.

In 1959 Robert Heilbroner, in *The Future as History*, wrote: "In the economic folklore of our country we still look back to 1929 not only as a year of great business prosperity but as a year of widespread and fundamental well-being. But when we examine the economy of 1929 critically, we find that the façade of business prosperity concealed an inner structure of widespread economic frailty."

This conclusion is clearly supported by the figures. If $3,000 in 1962 dollars is used as the poverty line, it

Table III-2   *Distribution of families and incomes by income (in 1962 dollars) 1929, 1947, and 1962*

Income level	1929	1947	1962
Under $3,000	51%	30%	21%
Between $3,000 and $6,000	34	40	31
Between $6,000 and $8,000	7	14	18
Between $8,000 and $10,000	3	7	11
$10,000 and over	5	9	19

Jeanette M. Fitzwilliams, "Size Distribution of Income in 1962," *Survey of Current Business*, April, 1963, Table 3. Figures for the under $3,000 group are based on unpublished data.

can be noted that thirty years ago about half of the families and individuals lived at levels that would be regarded as substandard today. This number may be somewhat overstated because of the inclusion of unrelated individuals, but it is not grossly out of line. Of course even today there are large numbers trying to get by on very little, but the proportion at this low level has been more than cut in half. In 1962 only about one-fifth of the families and individuals had incomes under $3,000.

The figures at the other end of the income scale show why ours is called an affluent society. In 1962 about one family out of every five had an income over $10,000. In many cases this high an income is achieved only because the wife and the husband are both out working; but the income is there nonetheless and it is available for air conditioners, dishwashers, second cars, and prestige schools. Thirty years ago an income over $10,000 (in 1962 terms; much less as dollars were counted then) was achieved by only one family out of twenty.

Looking back, there is good reason to wonder why 1929 was ever regarded as the end of a golden age. Incomes fell during the depression, to be sure; but they didn't fall from any great heights. By modern standards, life in 1929 would be very trying, to say the least. Take for example a simple matter like electric power. Today electricity in the home is taken for granted as a more or less inalienable right of every American. Practically every home—on the farm as well as in the city—is electrified. Even on southern farms, ninety-eight out of every hundred homes have electricity. In 1930, nine out of every ten farm homes were without this "necessity." And the country was much more rural then than it is now.

A more striking example is provided by the presence of a toilet in the home. Figures are not available for 1930, but the information was collected ten years later in the census. As recently as 1940, about 10 percent of city homes and 90 percent of farms lacked toilet facilities within the structure. This is not Russia or China that is being described, but these United States only one generation ago. If the situation was that bad in 1940, think how much worse it was in 1929.

It was generally believed during the depression that the basic economic problem facing the United States was overproduction. More goods were being produced than could be consumed. This feeling was expressed by the most advanced thinkers of the age and by the top political leaders. President Roosevelt stated in a talk before the Commonwealth Club of San Francisco on September 23, 1932: "Our industrial plant is built; the problem just now is whether under existing conditions it is not overbuilt." It is easy to see, with the benefit of thirty years of hindsight, that there were vast unfilled needs in 1929. By modern standards it was anything but a golden age. In the sixties America is once again being faced by the specter of "overproduction" and serious questions are being raised in some quarters as to whether we can consume all that is being produced—especially after automation is in full bloom. Only time will answer this question; but it is sobering to see how drastically perspectives can change in a short period of time. One cannot help but wonder if thirty years from now we will look back at the sixties and ask why, in the presence of unused resources, there were so many unfilled needs—inadequate schools, overcrowded hospitals and institutions, poor roads.

Long-term changes in income shares

Real incomes are higher in the United States than they are anywhere else in the world. Moreover, as demonstrated in the opening chapter, incomes are about as evenly distributed in the United States as they are in Great Britain and more evenly distributed than in most other countries for which such figures are available. Yet some critics complain that too few are getting too much. Gabriel Kolko is one such critic. He has several bones to pick with U.S. income distribution; but before we get to the heart of his argument his point of view should be examined. He states that his work is an analysis of social class and income distribution. "Depth and seriousness," he says, "have not been sacrificed for the superficial or the unproved." However, later on he writes, "Steaks are standard fare in the upper-income ranks: hamburger—which now accounts for one-quarter of beef consumption as opposed to one-tenth before World War II—is the staple of the luckier among the lower-income groups." Is this true? As you will see below, Kolko's statement is misleading. It is a minor point, to be sure, but it does indicate bias that permeates the book.

According to the Department of Agriculture, Kolko has understated the use of hamburger among American families. A food study conducted by the department in 1955 shows that 30 percent of all beef used in homes is in the form of ground beef or hamburger. The report also shows that about the same proportion is used as steak. So far, so good. Kolko still has his point. However, when beef consumption by income levels is examined, the differences do not appear to bear out his claims. About 31 percent of the beef used by families with incomes under $2,000 was hamburger as compared with 26 percent for families with incomes between $8,000 and $10,000. These facts suggest that American families at all income levels like their beef in the form of hamburgers, preferably burned on a backyard grill and mixed with charcoal, ashes, and flies.

Now let's look at the use of steak. Overall about one-third of the beef consumed in the home was in the form of steak. About 25 percent of the beef consumed by families with incomes under $2,000 was in the form of steak as compared with 37 percent for families with incomes between $8,000 and $10,000. There is a difference to be sure; but hardly one that merits the strong language Kolko has used. What other society, except perhaps Argentina, can Kolko point to where so much beef is consumed by the lowest income families and one-fourth of it in the form of steak?

Many of the other figures Kolko uses can be torn to pieces in the same way, but let's get to his main point. Kolko claims that "A radically unequal distribution of income has been characteristic of the American social structure since at least 1910, and despite minor year-to-year fluctuations in the shares of the income tenths, no significant trend toward income equality has appeared." The first part of this statement is entirely subjective and is not really subject to debate. As Professor Tawney once said, "One cannot argue with the choice of a soul; and if men like that kind of dog, then that is the kind of dog they like." The international comparison of Chapter I at least provides a framework against which our own performance can be measured and it does not make us look bad at all.

But the second part of the statement is subject to some verification and it is simply incorrect, even on the basis of the figures used by Kolko to support it. His figures for 1910–37, incidentally, were considered so inaccurate that they were deleted by a panel of experts from the joint Social Science Research Council–Census Bureau source book, *Historical Statistics of the United States, Colonial Times to 1957*, even though they had been included in an earlier version of that book.

According to Kolko's figures, the share of income received by the highest tenth of income recipients was 39 percent in 1921 and 1929, 34 percent in 1941, and 28 percent in 1950. He then denies the reality of this apparent leveling out. Kolko dismisses the figures for 1921 and 1929 without further explanation as representing exceptional years. He then concludes that the difference between the prewar and postwar figures can be eliminated when the latter are "corrected to allow for their exclusion of all forms of income in kind and the very substantial understatement of income by the wealthy." To dismiss the figures for the years with peak concentration as exceptional is the height of arbitrariness, particularly when there is evidence that the figures for 1921

33

and 1929 did not differ by more than a percentage point or two from any other year during the twenties. These were not exceptional years by any means.

But let us look further. Let's examine some figures that have been adjusted to include many types of income "in kind" that Kolko says are missing from the data and that have also been adjusted for underreporting of income. These figures are shown in Table III-3. They do not include various items which accrue primarily to the wealthy and which Kolko thinks should be added: notably expense accounts, capital gains, and undistributed profits. Also excluded from the figures, but not mentioned by Kolko, are fringe benefits such as life insurance, medical care, health insurance, and pension plans as well as the value of government services (which have been increasing rapidly in recent years and are widely distributed throughout the population). There is no sound way of knowing how these different types of hidden income offset each other in their impact on the entire distribution and we are clearly searching in muddy water at this point. Limited evidence suggests that the picture would not be drastically changed if capital gains and undistributed profits were added to the totals. A study published several years ago by members of the Office of Business Economics of the Department of Commerce showed that incomes were more equally distributed in the post–World War II period than in 1929 even when allowance was made for undistributed profits. A more recent study by the Department of Commerce shows that the addition of capital gains to the distribution increases the share received by the top 5 percent of the families and individuals by less than a percentage point.

Thus, even when "hidden income" is taken into account, the figures reflect the very trend toward income equality that Kolko denies. During the depression of the

Table III-3	*Percent of income received by each fifth of families and individuals and by top 5%*				
Families and individuals ranked from lowest to highest	1929	1935	1941	1944	1961
Lowest fifth ⎱	13%	⎰ 4%	4%	5%	5%
Second fifth ⎰		⎱ 9	10	11	11
Middle fifth	14	14	15	16	16
Fourth fifth	19	21	22	22	23
Highest fifth	54	52	49	46	45
Top 5%	30	27	24	21	20

U.S. Bureau of the Census, *Historical Statistics of the United States, Colonial Times to 1957*, p. 166, and Jeanette M. Fitzwilliams; see Table III-2.

thirties there was a distinct drop in the share of the income received by the upper income groups. In 1929, the last year of the prosperous twenties, the top 5 percent of the families and individuals received nearly one-third of the income. Their share dropped during the depression and amounted to about one-fourth of the income at the outbreak of World War II. During the war years there was a further decline and their share dropped to 21 percent in 1944. Since that time there has been no significant change in the percent of income received by the wealthiest group. The stability of income distribution during the past twenty years is a matter of some concern that has been generally overlooked by students in the field.

This aspect of the problem is explored in greater detail in the next chapter.

The trend described for the top twentieth applies to the top fifth as well. But now let's look at the bottom groups. In 1935, the poorest fifth of the families and individuals received only 4 percent of the income. Their share rose to 5 percent in 1944 and has remained at that level ever since. The stability since 1944 of the shares received by each of the other quintiles is equally striking.

The figures cited are for income before taxes. Since the wealthiest families pay a large share of the taxes, their share might be expected to be smaller on an after-tax basis. It is, but not by as much as one would guess. In recent years the wealthiest twentieth received 20 percent of the nation's income before taxes and about 18 percent of the income after federal individual income tax payments were deducted. The graduated income tax falls more heavily on the upper income groups than do most other major tax measures. It is, therefore, not surprising that the share of income received by the wealthy is decreased when individual income tax payments are deducted. It is a fact, however, that this tax accounted for only about 40 percent of the $113 billion collected in 1960 by the federal, state, and local governments. Many of the other taxes, like the sales tax, are paid disproportionately by the lower income groups. When all tax payments are taken into account, there is a real question as to whether taxes have a significant effect on the equalization of income.

CHAPTER IV

What's happening to our social revolution?

A myth has been created in the United States that incomes are gradually becoming more evenly distributed. This view is held by prominent economists of both major political parties. It is also shared by the editors of the influential mass media.

Arthur F. Burns, chief economist for the Eisenhower Administration, stated in 1951 that "the transformation in the distribution of our national income . . . may already be counted as one of the great social revolutions of history." Paul Samuelson, one of President Kennedy's leading economic advisers, stated in 1961 that "the American income pyramid is becoming less unequal." Several major stories on this subject have appeared in the *New York Times*, and the editors of *Fortune* magazine announced ten years ago: "Though not a head has been raised aloft on a pikestaff, nor a railway station seized, the U.S. has been for some time now in a revolution."

In the preceding chapter, several basic facts were presented regarding trends in the inequality of income distribution in the United States. It was shown that there has been no appreciable change in income shares for nearly twenty years. This question will now be examined a little more intensively.

Despite the existence of much poverty in the United States, there is general agreement that real levels of living are much higher than they were only ten years ago and that the prospects for future increases are very good.

37

Since conditions are improving you may wonder why it is important to consider the gap between the rich and the poor. Isn't it enough that the *amount* of income received by the poor has gone up substantially? Why be concerned about their share? Many who have thought about this problem seriously regard the *share* as the critical factor. When Karl Marx, for example, spoke about the inevitability of increasing misery among workers under capitalism he had a very special definition of misery in mind. Sumner Slichter, in summarizing the Marxian position on this point, states: "Marx held that wages depend upon the customary wants of the laboring class. Wages, so determined, might rise in the long run. Hence, Marx conceded that real wages *might* rise, but not the relative share of labor. Even if real wages rose, misery would grow, according to Marx, since workers would be worse off relative to capitalists."

Arnold Toynbee has approached the problem of income shares in still another way. He notes that minimum standards of living have been raised considerably and will continue to be raised in the future, but he observes that this rise has not stopped us from "demanding social justice; and the unequal distribution of the world's goods between a privileged minority and an underprivileged majority has been transformed from an unavoidable evil to an intolerable injustice."

In other words "needs" stem not so much from what we lack as from what our neighbors have. Veblen called this trait our "pecuniary standard of living" and modern economists refer to it as the "relative income hypothesis," but it all comes back to the same thing. Except for those rare souls who have hitched their wagons to thoughts rather than things, there is no end to "needs." So long as there are people who have more, others will "need" more. If this is indeed the basis for human behavior, then obviously the gap between the rich and the poor cannot be ignored, however high the *minimum* levels of living may be raised.

Although the figures show no appreciable change in income shares for nearly twenty years, the problem is complex and there is much that the statistics cannot show. It is conceivable, for example, that a proportional increase in everybody's real income means more to the poor than to the rich. The gap in "living levels" may have closed more than the gap in incomes. Even if exact comparisons are not possible, many believe that by satisfying the most urgent and basic needs of the poor, there has been some "leveling up" in the comforts of life.

Other examples of a similar nature can be cited. The extension of government services benefits low-income families more than those who have higher incomes—by providing better housing, more adequate medical care, and improved educational facilities. The increase in paid vacations has surely brought a more equal distribution of leisure time—a good that is almost as precious as money. Finally, improved working conditions—air conditioning, better light, mechanization of routine work—has undoubtedly reduced the painfulness of earning a living more for manual workers than for those who are in higher paid and more responsible positions.

When allowance is made for all of these factors, and for many others not mentioned, it may well be that some progress has been made during recent years in diminishing the inequality of levels of living. But it is hard to know how much allowance to make and our judgments could be wrong. Most opinions regarding changes in inequality, including those held by professional economists, are based on statistical measures of income rather than on philosophical concepts. With all their limitations, the income figures may well serve as a first approximation of changes in welfare. These figures show that the share of income received by the lower income groups has not changed for twenty years. Let us look at some other evidence that supports this view and then examine the implications of the findings.

White-nonwhite income differentials are not narrowing

The narrowing of income differentials between whites and nonwhites (92 percent of whom are Negroes) is sometimes cited as evidence of a trend toward equalization. Several years ago, Professor Joseph Kahl of Washington University stated: "The poorest section of the country, the South, and the poorest group in the country, the Negroes, made the greatest gains of all."

What are the facts? Surely one would expect a change here in view of the major relocation of the Negro population in recent years. Migration and technological change during the past twenty years have altered the role of the nonwhite from a southern farmhand or sharecropper to an industrial worker. In 1940, about three-fourths of all nonwhites lived in the South and were largely engaged in agriculture. By 1950, the proportion residing in the South had dropped to about two-thirds, and today it is down to a little more than half. Even in the South, nonwhites are now more concentrated in urban areas than ever before.

The change in the occupations of nonwhite males tells the story of their altered economic role even more dramatically. Twenty years ago, four out of every ten nonwhites who worked were laborers or sharecroppers on southern farms. At present, less than two out of every ten are employed in agriculture, and about five out of ten work as unskilled or semiskilled workers at nonfarm jobs. The change in the occupational status of nonwhites has been accompanied by a marked rise in educational attainment, proportionately far greater than for whites. In 1940, young white males averaged four years more of schooling than nonwhites in the same age group. Today the gap has been narrowed to one and a half years.

The income gap between whites and nonwhites did narrow during World War II. During the last decade, however, it shows some evidence of having widened again (see Table IV-1 and pictograph). The census statistics demonstrate this dismaying fact.

In 1947, the median wage or salary income for nonwhite workers was 54 percent of that received by the whites. In 1962, the ratio was almost identical (55 percent). Prior to 1947 there was a substantial reduction in the earnings gap between whites and nonwhites. In view of the stability of the earnings gap during the postwar period, however, the reduction during the war years cannot be viewed as part of a continuing process, but rather as a phenomenon closely related to war-induced shortages of unskilled labor and government regulations such as those of the War Labor Board designed generally to raise the incomes of lower paid workers, and to an economy operating at full tilt.

This conclusion is reinforced by details of the 1960 census which show that in the twenty-six states (including the District of Columbia) which have 100,000 or more Negroes, the ratio of Negro to white income for males increased between 1949 and 1959 in two states (District of Columbia and Florida) and it was unchanged in two others (New Jersey and Oklahoma). In every other state there was a widening of the gap between the incomes of whites and Negroes and in some cases it was fairly substantial.

Table IV-1	The income gap: white vs. nonwhite male workers aged 14 and over, in 1939, and 1947 to 1962

Year	White	Nonwhite	Nonwhite as percent of white
All persons with wage or salary income:			
1939	$1,112	$ 460	41%
1947	2,357	1,279	54
1948	2,711	1,615	60
1949	2,735	1,367	50
1950	2,982	1,828	61
1951	3,345	2,060	62
1952	3,507	2,038	58
1953	3,760	2,233	59
1954	3,754	2,131	57
1955	3,986	2,342	59
1956	4,260	2,396	56
1957	4,396	2,436	55
1958	4,596	2,652	58
1959	4,902	2,844	58
1960	5,137	3,075	60
1961	5,287	3,015	57
1962	5,462	3,023	55

Year	White	Nonwhite	Nonwhite as percent of white
Year-round full-time workers with wage or salary income:			
1939	$1,419	$ 639	45
1955	4,458	2,831	64
1956	4,710	2,912	62
1957	4,950	3,137	63
1958	5,186	3,368	65
1959	5,456	3,339	61
1960	5,662	3,789	67
1961	5,880	3,883	66
1962	6,025	3,799	63

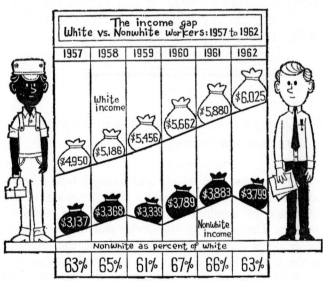

U.S. Bureau of the Census, *Current Population Reports —Consumer Income*, Series P-60, annual issues.

Professional and managerial Workers — Craftsmen

1939 $1,986 | 1950 $3,890 | 1961 $6,821 | 1939 $1,309 | 1950 $3,405 | 1961 $5,527

Men's income by Occupation in 1939, 1950, and 1961

Occupational differentials in earnings are not narrowing

One of the most widely and strongly held misconceptions about income concerns the narrowing of the difference in earnings between skilled and unskilled workers. The prevailing view holds that the decrease in the earnings gap between the skilled and the unskilled in the United States is part of a historical process that has been going on since the turn of the century. The Department of Labor reports that in 1907 the median earnings of skilled workers in manufacturing industries was about twice that received by unskilled workers. By the

Table IV-2a.

Table IV-2b	Men's income by occupation: percent change

Year	Professional and managerial workers	Craftsmen	Semiskilled factory workers	Service workers and nonfarm laborers
1939–61	243%	322%	331%	314%
1939–50	96	160	172	180
1950–61	75	62	59	48

U.S. Bureau of the Census, *Current Population Reports —Consumer Income*, Series P-60, Nos. 9 and 39 (for Tables IV-2a and IV-2b).

end of World War I, it was only 75 percent greater, and by the end of World War II only 55 percent greater. Thus, during a forty-year period, this income gap was reduced by about 50 percent, an average of about 1 percent per year.

Recent trends in income differentials between skilled and unskilled workers are shown in the pictograph (Table iv-2a) and Table iv-2b. These figures represent the median wages and salaries received during the year in the major occupation groups for men. Women are excluded because their earnings are highly influenced by the fact that a large proportion of them work intermittently rather than full time.

There was not too much variation among occupation groups in the rate of income growth during the entire twenty-two-year period. The average income for most of the occupations quadrupled. But an examination of the growth rates for two different periods, 1939–50, and 1950–61, reveals striking differences.

During the decade that included World War II, the lower paid occupations made the greatest relative gains in average income. Thus, laborers and service workers (waiters, barbers, janitors, and the like), two of the lowest paid groups among nonfarm workers, had increases of about 180 percent. The gains for craftsmen, who are somewhat higher paid, was 160 percent; professional and managerial workers, the highest paid workers of all, had the lowest relative gains—96 percent.

During the past decade the picture has been reversed. Laborers and service workers made the smallest relative gains, 48 percent; craftsmen had increases of 62 percent, and the professional and managerial workers had the greatest gains of all, 75 percent. The narrowing of the income gap between the skilled and the unskilled, the high-paid and the low-paid workers, which was evident up to and including the war years, has stopped during the past decade and the trend seems to be moving in the opposite direction.

The above figures are national averages in which all industries and regions are combined. They are very useful for identifying major trends, but they can also be very misleading because they average together so many different things. It is important to examine the figures for a particular industry in a particular region to get a better understanding of the underlying trends. The primary and fabricated metals industries have been selected for this purpose. The same analysis was also made for about ten other major American industries and the results are generally the same as those presented below.

About 2,200,000 men were engaged in the production of metals or the fabrication of metal products in 1960. This employment was about equally divided between production and fabrication.

The production of primary metals consists of three major components: blast furnaces and steel mills with about 600,000 men; other primary iron and steel works (mostly foundries) with about 300,000 men; and primary nonferrous metal (mostly aluminum) plants, with about 300,000 men. The iron and steel industry is highly concentrated in the Northeast and North Central states and within these states it can be further pinpointed to the following areas: Pittsburgh-Youngstown, Cleveland-Detroit, and Chicago.

The fabrication industry has a similar geographic distribution. About one-third of the workers are employed in the Northeastern states and a somewhat larger proportion are in the North Central region. This industry is divided into several major components, two of which are dominant and account for about nine-tenths of the employment. The largest component manufac-

47

| 260,000 | 220,000 | 650,000 | 780,000 | 540,000 | 660,000 | 340,000 | 550,000 |

Men employed in the metal industries: 1950 and 1960

Table IV-3. *U.S. Census of Population: 1960*, Vol. II, *Occupation by Industry*, Table 2; and *U.S. Census of Population: 1950*, Vol. II, Table 84.

tures structural metal products—a miscellany ranging from bridge sections to bins, metal doors, windows, etc. It employs 200,000 men. The second major category, called "miscellaneous fabricated metal products," makes everything from dog chains to missiles and employs 700,000 men.

An examination of employment in this industry shows that the total number of workers increased by 24 percent between 1950 and 1960. Professional, managerial, and other white-collar workers increased 62 percent; skilled and semiskilled production workers increased by about 20 percent, but unskilled laborers decreased 9 percent. Thus, despite the general rise in employment and output in this industry, there was a drop in the demand for unskilled labor.

In view of these changes in the demand for labor in this industry, what happened to earnings? The figures for the eight major metal-producing and fabricating states are shown in Table IV-4. The states are shown in order of the size of their employment in this industry. They accounted for nearly three-fourths of the entire employment in this industry in 1960. The actual dollar earnings for unskilled, semiskilled, and all other workers (largely craftsmen and white-collar workers) for 1939, 1949, and 1959 are shown in the first part of the table; percentage changes are shown in the second part. It is the latter figures that are of greatest interest because they show which groups made the greatest relative gains. There are some differences in the definition of earnings for each of the years shown, but they are not believed to create serious distortions in the figures for these workers.

In all states except Ohio and California, unskilled workers in this industry made greater relative gains than the semiskilled between 1939–49. Similar figures are not available for the higher paid "other" workers for 1939. Thus there was a tendency toward a narrowing of earnings differentials in this industry between 1939–49. But, during the decade 1949–59, the reverse was true. In every state there was a widening of differentials, with the highest paid "other" workers making the greatest relative gains, followed by the semiskilled workers and then the unskilled. In Pennsylvania, for example, laborers had a 63 percent increase in earnings between 1949–59, semiskilled operatives had a 66 percent increase, and professional, managerial, and other white-collar workers had a 75 percent increase. The same general pattern of wage movement was found in each of the other states shown.

49

Table IV-4   *Regional differences in income of men in the metal industries in 1939, 1949, and 1959*

State	Laborers			Operatives			Other workers	
	1939	*1949*	*1959*	*1939*	*1949*	*1959*	*1949*	*1959*
Pennsylvania	$ 947	$2,414	$3,939	$1,153	$2,767	$4,597	$3,220	$5,624
Ohio	1,006	2,403	4,077	1,091	2,841	4,885	3,367	5,920
California	1,056	2,411	4,136	1,231	2,814	5,002	3,639	6,866
Illinois	950	2,506	4,448	1,124	2,931	5,034	3,517	6,321
New York	918	2,503	3,940	1,060	2,703	4,458	3,318	5,796
Michigan	962	2,645	4,134	1,150	2,997	4,726	3,691	6,246
Indiana	1,074	2,526	4,054	1,286	2,918	4,897	3,454	5,792
Alabama	701	2,032	3,565	887	2,316	4,301	3,073	5,864

Amount of earnings

State	Percent increase, 1939–49		Percent increase, 1949–59		
	Laborers	Operatives	Laborers	Operatives	Other workers
Pennsylvania	155%	140%	63%	66%	75%
Ohio	139	160	70	72	76
California	128	129	72	78	89
Illinois	164	161	77	72	80
New York	173	155	57	65	75
Michigan	175	161	56	58	69
Indiana	134	127	60	68	68
Alabama	190	161	75	86	91

U.S. Census of Population: 1960, Detailed Characteristics,
Tables 124 and 130; *U.S. Census of Population: 1950.*
Vol. II, Tables 78 and 86; and *U.S. Census of Population: 1940,* Vol. III, Table 16.

Where do we go from here?

There was a time, not too long ago, when economists did not look for changes in income distribution because they did not expect to find any. Indeed, the stability of the income curve was so striking that it was given a name, Pareto's Law, in honor of the economist who conducted some of the earliest statistical inquiries in this field.

Pareto believed that the distribution of income is fixed and that regardless of changes in economic conditions, short of a revolutionary change from a competitive to a collectivist society, the distribution of income is the same in all places and at all times.

Statistical studies in recent years have so thoroughly demolished Pareto's notions that we have now come to look for change where no change exists. The facts show that our "social revolution" ended nearly twenty years ago; yet important segments of the American public, many of them highly placed government officials and prominent educators, think and act as though it were a continuing process. Intelligent public policy demands that things be seen as they are, not as they were.

The stability of income distribution, particularly during the fifties, could be related to the fact that the decade was dominated by a political philosophy committed to stability rather than change. In a different climate income differentials might narrow further. This could be accomplished through legislation designed to raise the levels of living of the poor: expansion of unemployment insurance benefits, federal aid to dependent children of the unemployed, liberalization of social security benefits, increase in the minimum wage and extension of its coverage, federal aid under the Area Redevelopment Act to revitalize the economies of areas with large and persistent unemployment.

In opposition to political factors that seem to favor equalization, there are some very stubborn economic factors that seem to be headed in quite the other direction. For many years now unskilled workers have been a declining part of the American labor force. This fact has been documented over and over again. Between 1940 and 1950 and again between 1950 and 1960 only one nonfarm occupation group for men—laborers—declined in number at a time when all other groups were increasing. Their income changed erratically. Laborers had the greatest relative income gains during the forties and the smallest relative gains during the fifties. This could mean that unskilled labor was in very short supply during World War II, with millions of young men away in the armed forces and the economy working at full steam. This pressure, with a little help from the government, forced wage rates up more for unskilled workers than for other workers. Since the fifties, on the other hand, there is evidence that the supply of unskilled labor has far exceeded the demand. As a result the unskilled are finding it increasingly difficult to locate jobs and many who are employed live in constant fear of being replaced by machines. Moreover, the overabundance of these workers has prevented their wages from keeping pace with the others; thus the gap between the earnings of skilled and unskilled has widened.

The American economy has been plagued by relatively high unemployment since late 1957. According to the Joint Economic Committee, which has studied this problem in some detail, it is still premature to attribute this unemployment to the technological changes that are rapidly reshaping the economy. However, there can be no doubt that many thousands of unskilled workers in farming, manufacturing, mining, and railroads have been permanently displaced by machines and that this trend will continue. The labor-union leaders who represent these workers certainly tend to view the problem in this light. Even if they do not qualify as impartial observers, they know how these economic developments are interpreted at the grass-roots level. The leader of the Transport Workers Union of America, Michael Quill, is one among many who have spoken out sharply. His words carry a defiant ring that has been virtually absent from the American scene for over twenty years. He stated: "Unless something is done to put people to work despite automation, they may get rough in this country and this country may have a real upheaval, a real turmoil." The increase in racial tension and juvenile delinquency during the past few years may be early manifestations of trouble to come.

Labor-union leaders are not the only ones who have shown a keen awareness of both the bogey and the boon of automation. Many who have given the matter serious thought find it conceivable that, in the absence of remedial action, this nation may soon be faced with an increase in the disparity of incomes. We may then discover that our "social revolution" has not only been marking time for nearly twenty years, but that it is beginning to move backward. Justice William O. Douglas has spoken out eloquently on this subject in the pamphlet *Freedom of the Mind:* "We have a surplus of everything—including unemployed people; and the hundreds of unemployed and unemployable will increase if technology continues to be our master. We have a surplus of food and millions of hungry people at home as well as abroad. When the machine displaces man and does most of the work, who will own the machines and receive the rich dividends? Are we on the threshold of re-entering the world of feudalism which Europe left in the 15th and 16th centuries and which is fastened on much of the Middle East today?"

CHAPTER V

Look around—the poor are still here

Poverty amidst plenty

"Ye have the poor with you always." So it says in the Bible and so it is. Truer words were never written. The proof can be found right here at home. One report found that in this, the richest of all countries, 40 percent of the families live in poverty or deprivation. In fact that is the title of a study published in 1962, *Poverty and Deprivation in the U.S.—The Plight of Two-Fifths of a Nation*. This is no phony Communist propaganda, nor the wild charges of a radical reformer. These are hard-boiled statistical "facts" prepared by Leon Keyserling, chief economic counselor to President Truman and former head of the Council of Economic Advisers.

Does it seem strange that in 1962 Keyserling found that two-fifths of the families were poor when even during the depression President Roosevelt found that only one-third of the nation was ill-housed, ill-clothed, and ill-fed? The amount of goods and services per capita has doubled since the early thirties. How then can there have been an increase in the proportion of families living at substandard levels? The answer is quite simple. It all depends on how high you set your standard. In 1889, a study was made of poverty in London, *Life and Labour of the People*. It showed that about one-third of the people lived in poverty. During the depression a similar

56

study was made in the United States. It also showed that about one-third of the people lived in poverty. Recent statistics for American cities prepared by the Bureau of Labor Statistics also point to the conclusion that about one-third of the people have incomes insufficient to maintain a decent level of living. The clear meaning of these findings is that as incomes go up "needs" also go up, evidently in such a way as to leave a large proportion of the population at substandard levels.

The term "poverty" connotes hunger; but this is not what is meant in discussions about poverty in America. Harlan County, Kentucky, is about as poor a county as you will find in this country. If you remember the depression, you're almost sure to remember Harlan County, Kentucky. It was the scene of many bloody mine union battles during the thirties. These battles are commemorated in a union song that goes something like this:

> They say in Harlan County
> There are no neutrals there.
> You either be a Union man
> Or a thug for J. H. Blair.
>> Which side are you on?
>> Which side are you on?

Harlan County was poor in the thirties and it still is. The clearest sign of its poverty is the fact that people are leaving in droves. Half the people who lived there in 1950 were gone by 1960. And those who remained did not live well by any means. Two-thirds of the homes were substandard. Half lacked baths, inside toilets, and other conveniences that are regarded as essential for modern living. One-fourth even lacked running water in the home. By present-day American standards they are poor, poor, poor.

But let's probe a little deeper:

88% have washing machines
67% have TV
42% have a telephone
59% have a car

It is quite evident that even in this poor American community there are many of the trappings of an affluent society. Some families have washing machines but no running water. They carry water from a well to a machine to get their clothes washed. Three-fifths of the families have cars. Many of the cars may be jalopies, but even a jalopy costs $500 or more a year to run. Two-thirds of the families have TV sets. They may not be the latest models. The fact that they are there, however, immediately points to a distinction between the American poor and the starving poor in India or China.

There are many different definitions of poverty. According to Keyserling's definition in the study cited above, an American family faces stark poverty if its income is under $4,000 and it is deprived with an income of less than $6,000. In the figures shown on pages 62–63, the poor are defined as the families in the bottom fifth of the income distribution. In 1960, these families had cash incomes under $3,000. (Since Keyserling's figure includes noncash income, the two numbers are not as different as they might at first appear.) This definition of poverty is arbitrary. It includes among the poor some families that do not really belong there and it excludes some that should be counted. One justification for the use of this definition is its use by a congressional committee, which concluded that in 1957 the lowest fifth of the families were in "low-income status." There is no reason to believe that this proportion would have changed by the time the census was taken in 1960. The term "poor" as employed here is synonymous with "low-income status," "bottom income groups" and other euphemistic phrases that are often used to describe poverty.

Who is poor?—A summary view

Who are the American poor? How did they get that way? How have their characteristics changed over time? At this point, the problem will be examined broadly. A more detailed appraisal is presented in the following section. There are many reasons for poverty, but some are much more important than others and they appear with remarkable regularity in the studies that have been made.

A few of the most significant characteristics of the poorest fifth of the families in 1951 and 1960 are shown in Table v-1. The key fact to notice is how little these characteristics have changed in the past decade. Of course, this does not mean that those who were poor in 1951 were still poor in 1960. If tags could be put on people so they could be followed through life, you would surely find that some who were higher up on the income scale in 1951 have dropped down relative to others because of retirement, widowhood, divorce, illness, and many other factors. Conversely, many who were poor in 1951 have undoubtedly moved up. This would be particularly true of young couples that were just starting out ten years earlier.

The kinds of forces involved in the movement of families in and out of poverty over a period of time can be seen in a particular case—Mr. and Mrs. Bacon of New York City. In 1950, the Bacons (the name is fictitious but the case is real) were interviewed by a welfare agency in New York City as one of one hundred poor families, for the Joint Committee on the Economic Report. The facts stated here are those shown in the report *Making Ends Meet on Less Than $2,000 a Year.*

Mr. Bacon at age thirty-eight was a temporary postal worker who made $1,820 in 1949. This was the total income he had to support his wife and three children aged six, four, and one. The family lived in a low-income housing project, where they had a two-bedroom apartment costing $38 a month, utilities included. They were eligible for a three-bedroom apartment but did not apply for it in order to save on the rent. The parents' bedroom was shared by their year-old daughter; the two boys had the other bedroom.

Mr. Bacon had quit school at sixteen. At seventeen he had been convicted of a petty theft and put on probation. He had knocked about from job to job, working as a construction laborer before he took the temporary job in the post office. He was a heavy drinker and, according to the social worker who reported the case, an unstable person who occasionally deserted his family.

Mrs. Bacon was more responsible than her husband, but she was having a very difficult time keeping the family together. She was a high school graduate but was unable to fulfill her plans for a nursing career. She had worked in a factory and in a hospital for a few years before her marriage. She was basically healthy, but at age thirty-seven all her upper teeth had been removed and she could not afford dentures. According to the social worker, Mrs. Bacon did a good job as a housewife, but she did not fully appreciate the seriousness of her plight. The apartment was described as pleasant and clean, with colorful curtains hanging on the windows. Mrs. Bacon managed her money well, although with only $20 a week to spend on food, cheese often had to be substituted for meat. The relationship between the parents was strained, but Mrs. Bacon thought her husband would stay home more if they could only get a television set.

The tension between the parents seriously affected the oldest child. He was asthmatic and had to miss school one day each week to go to a clinic for treatments. At his young age, he had already been labeled a problem child in school and had to be taken to a psychologist.

What happens to a family like the Bacons? The seeds of poverty were planted here, not only for the present generation, but for future generations as well. Unfortunately, the family was not followed over the years, so there is no way of knowing just what became of them. Still it is interesting to speculate. Mr. Bacon had little schooling, no vocational training or skill, and he drank. None of these traits are conducive to regular employment or high income and it is likely that he has had neither. The Bacons may well be one of those families that would be counted among the poor at any time, but this is not necessarily the case. Life is complex and almost anything is possible.

In the years since the Bacons were first interviewed, much could have happened. The oldest child was twenty in 1963 and he could have been out working and contributing to the support of the family. If he had a factory job, he could be adding substantially to the family income. Moreover, the youngest Bacon child would be fifteen in 1963, if no other children were born. This would leave Mrs. Bacon free to accept employment and even a part-time job could pull the family above the poverty line. By considering only a few of the things that might have happened to this one family, you can see the factors that might cause the movement of families into or out of poverty over a period of time.

The figures in the pictograph (Table v-1) summarize some of the characteristics of poor families in

Aged

1951
31%

1960
31%

No Worker
in family

1951
25%

1960
28%

Who are the Poor?...Selected characteristics

1951 and 1960. They suggest strongly that, although some families entered the ranks of the poor during the decade and others moved up the income ladder, on the average the same *kinds* of people were poor throughout the period.

Even these few figures present a very graphic picture of the factors associated with poverty. You can see a predominance of conditions that are traditionally associated with poverty—old age, broken homes, non-

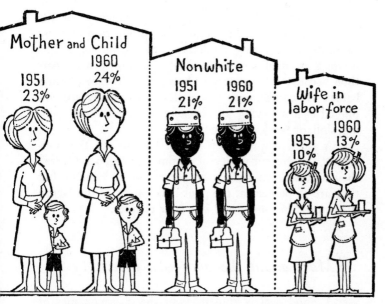

Table v-1. U.S. Bureau of the Census, *How Our In-Come Is Divided*, Graphic Pamphlet No. 2, 1963. In this table a family may be counted more than once.

whites, and unemployment or failure to work for other reasons.

Perhaps the most distinctive characteristic of the poor is their low productivity. Most of these families are headed by persons who cannot command a high income because of age or lack of training or work experience. The aged are a case in point. They form the single largest block at the bottom. Since most of them are in retirement and are living on pensions, it is to be expected that their incomes will lag behind the working population.

The economic problems of broken families are not too dissimilar from those of the aged. These families are the product of divorce, desertion, illegitimacy, or the death of a husband. In a very large proportion of these cases, there are young children present in the home. The mothers are unable to work at all or can only work part time because they must stay home to take care of their babies. Of course, even when they work, many are employed in low-paying jobs because of their lack of training, skill, or work experience.

A third major group at the bottom are the non-whites, the great majority of whom are Negroes. Overall they represent only about 10 percent of all families; but they are 21 percent of the poor. The plight of the Negro is discussed in some detail in a later chapter.

More about the poor—an inventory

A good deal is known about the characteristics of poor families from small surveys that are made each year. But the 1960 census provides a much closer look at this group. At the time of the last census, there were nearly ten million families with incomes under $3,000. They were the poorest fifth of all families. What were they like? A very detailed statistical profile is provided in Table v-2. To these numbers must be added several million unrelated individuals with very low incomes and very poor prospects, who are not shown in this table.

Much about the American poor can be pinpointed by lumping the detailed figures of Table v-2 into five major groups, as in the pictograph (Table v-3). In this classification, each family with a 1959 income less than $3,000 is counted only once, although the classification factors seem to overlap. That is, all farm families—whether or not they are aged, fatherless, or nonwhite—are counted in Group I. All families that are aged but *not* farmers are counted in Group II, whether or not they also are fatherless or nonwhite, and so on.

Table v-2	*Families with income less than $3,000 in 1959*		
Characteristic	Total	White	Nonwhite
Total families	9,650,000	7,615,000	2,035,000
Husband-wife	7,207,000	5,910,000	1,297,000
Head under 35	1,582,000	1,230,000	352,000
Head 35 to 64	3,264,000	2,555,000	709,000
Head 65 and over	2,361,000	2,125,000	236,000
Other male head	368,000	282,000	86,000
Head under 35	47,000	32,000	15,000
Head 35 to 64	178,000	131,000	47,000
Head 65 and over	143,000	119,000	24,000
Female head	2,075,000	1,423,000	652,000
Head under 35	530,000	318,000	212,000
Head 35 to 64	1,096,000	747,000	349,000
Head 65 and over	449,000	358,000	91,000
URBAN AND RURAL NONFARM			
All families	8,080,000	6,279,000	1,801,000
Husband-wife	5,810,000	4,709,000	1,101,000
Head under 35	1,366,000	1,051,000	315,000
Head 35 to 64	2,392,000	1,810,000	581,000
Head 65 and over	2,053,000	1,848,000	205,000

Table v-2 (*Cont.*)

Characteristic	Total	White	Nonwhite
Other male head	299,000	223,000	75,000
Head under 35	43,000	28,000	14,000
Head 35 to 64	138,000	98,000	40,000
Head 65 and over	118,000	97,000	21,000
Female head	1,971,000	1,347,000	625,000
Head under 35	522,000	314,000	209,000
Head 35 to 64	1,039,000	708,000	332,000
Head 65 and over	410,000	325,000	84,000
RURAL FARM			
All families	1,570,000	1,336,000	234,000
Husband-wife	1,397,000	1,201,000	196,000
Head under 35	216,000	179,000	37,000
Head 35 to 64	872,000	744,000	128,000
Head 65 and over	309,000	278,000	31,000
Other male head	70,000	59,000	11,000
Head under 35	5,000	4,000	1,000
Head 35 to 64	40,000	34,000	7,000
Head 65 and over	25,000	21,000	3,000
Female head	103,000	76,000	27,000
Head under 35	8,000	4,000	3,000
Head 35 to 64	57,000	40,000	17,000
Head 65 and over	38,000	32,000	7,000

U.S. Census of Population: 1960, Detailed Characteristics, United States Summary, Table 224.

This technique is a useful sieving process that might be compared to the selection of hotel rooms for the different families. Imagine a series of five rooms lined up

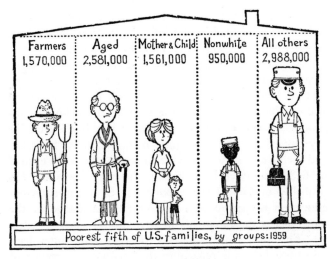

| Farmers 1,570,000 | Aged 2,581,000 | Mother & Child 1,561,000 | Nonwhite 950,000 | All others 2,988,000 |

Poorest fifth of U.S. families, by groups: 1959

Table v-3. Derived from Table v-2.

consecutively and each connected by a door. A family enters the first room. If it is headed by a farmer, it stays in that room regardless of any other characteristic it may have; otherwise it goes into the second room. The family remains in the second room only if the head is sixty-five years old or over, otherwise it goes into the third room. It stays in the third room only if it is headed by a woman, otherwise it goes into the fourth room. It stays in the fourth room only if it is nonwhite, otherwise it goes into the fifth room and remains there. After one family has been assigned to a room, a second one starts the procedure all over again and keeps going from room to room until it too finds its proper place. In this way all of the 9,650,000 families with incomes under $3,000 are classified into each of the five groups.

Before examining the groups individually, a word should be said about the reason for selecting them. If every family is to be counted in only one category, a decision must be made regarding the relative importance of each of the reasons why families are poor.

Consider, for example, the case of an elderly Negro farmer trying to scratch a living out of an unwilling plot of land. Why is he poor? Well, there are several reasons. In the first place, the land he is working is unproductive and could not provide a livelihood even for a younger and more energetic man. Secondly, he is old and feeble and may be unable to work efficiently even if he had productive land. Finally, he is a Negro and has probably never had the opportunity to obtain sufficient education to permit him to take full advantage of the most recent developments in agricultural science.

To assign a man like this to one group, some decision must be made regarding the relative importance of his many handicaps. The decision is subjective; but anyone who wants to can go back to the detailed figures and recast the numbers to suit himself. It probably will not make too much difference because the number of crucial variables is quite limited.

In the present grouping it was decided that farm residence takes precedence above all others. One reason for this judgment is that the cash income figures used here have less meaning for the farmers than for nonfarm groups because farmers often receive food and lodging in addition to their cash income. Also, trying to eke a living out of barren soil is probably a more important cause of poverty than any personal characteristics an individual may have. Moreover, if you live on a farm, the opportunities for more profitable employment elsewhere are often quite limited, although many farmers do have some nonfarm employment.

Age was used as the second major category. Most people over sixty-five years old are either unable to work

68

or they cannot find jobs under current conditions of employment. The resident of a city who is too old to work must live on savings, pensions, or handouts. It does not matter much if the individual is a man or a woman, white or nonwhite. The income will be quite low in any event.

The fatherless family was used as the third major category. The women who head these homes generally have trouble as a constant companion. They have responsibilities at home that prevent them from working full time; they lack the training that commands good wages. The family income will be low.

Families headed by a nonwhite male under sixty-five years old were classified in the fourth category. These families live in nonfarm areas, generally central cities, where jobs are available. They are also headed by men who are still in their productive ages. Their incomes should be high, but they are not. It is presumed that discrimination is one important reason why they are poor. In many cases, however, their poverty may be unrelated to the fact that they are nonwhite.

Finally, there are those families who are poor even though they do not seem to suffer from any of the obvious factors that cause poverty. Many of these families are Puerto Ricans and Mexicans, who are technically white but do not get the advantages that "whitehood" brings. Many other families are headed by men who are disabled, younger men who are just getting started, or by men who never did get started and never will because they simply lack what it takes to rise above minimum levels of living in this society. There are millions of fine, respectable, honest men whose native intelligence is quite low and who lack training to do any but the most menial work. They are poor because their productivity is low. This type of individual is likely to become an increasingly serious social problem. The situation was clearly stated by the editor of *Harper's* magazine in September, 1962: "It is perfectly clear to me, at least, why Mr. Kennedy hasn't been able to find jobs for our three or four million unemployed. The human race—or anyhow that sample of it located in North America—no longer fits the kind of society it has to live in. Our society just doesn't have any jobs for certain types of people. If it continues to develop along its present course, the number of such unemployables seems likely to grow rather rapidly."

Why they are poor

Low-income farmers

There were about one and a half million farm families with cash incomes under $3,000 in 1959. The great majority of these families had incomes under $2,000, so they would be considered poor even if a generous allowance were made for the imputed value of rent and food produced and consumed on the farm.

Only about one-quarter million of these families were nonwhite, so that the low-income farm population is no longer dominated by Negro sharecroppers. That was the case twenty years ago. Since then the Negroes have largely left the farms and they are more highly clustered in the centers of large cities.

Broken families are also scarce on farms. If a farm woman is left without a man, she will more likely than not remarry or give up the farm and seek other quarters. Thus the great bulk of the low-income farm residents are white families consisting of a husband, wife, and in many cases children. About half of these family heads are between forty-five and sixty-four years old and an equal number are under thirty-five or over sixty-five. At one time, this type of farm probably contained a much larger segment of the poor than it does today. The northward migration of the Negro and the magnetism of better job opportunities in the big cities have acted as a constant drain for the younger population on these farms. As a result, marginal farmers are dwindling as a proportion of the poor.

About one-half of these low-income farm families live in the South. In Alabama and Mississippi, half of the farm families have incomes under $2,000 a year. Farmers in the other parts of the South are not much better off. Michael Harrington in *The Other America* has aptly described rural areas in the South as "a belt of misery that runs from the Middle Atlantic coast to the South and to the West."

The reasons for farm poverty are about as varied as the poor themselves. There is no such thing as a "typical" case. And yet there are some aspects of farm poverty that can best be understood only in the context of a particular case (real but disguised).

In 1950, Jason and Luella Wood were interviewed in Kansas for the Joint Committee on the Economic Report. At the time, they operated a hundred-acre farm that they rented for one-half the crops. Mr. Wood raised corn and prairie hay, getting around twenty bushels of corn to the acre. He did not sell his share of the crops but kept it as livestock feed. For cash income, Mr. Wood raised chickens and sold cream to a local produce station. His net income after farm-operating expenses was $800.

The Woods raised almost all of their own foodstuff and spent only $125 during the year for store groceries. Their home was a forty-year-old seven-room house, livable but in need of many minor repairs. Wood and coal stoves were used for heating and cooking in winter, and kerosene was used in the summer. A pitcher pump in the kitchen supplied soft water from a cistern while a well some distance from the house provided drinking water. They had no electricity and used kerosene and gasoline lights and a battery-operated radio. Mrs. Wood made most of her clothes, many of them from feed bags, which were also used for tablecloths and curtains. The Woods did own a good car, bought secondhand.

Despite their very frugal living, the Woods spent every cent of the $800 they made. The only reserves they had were $300 in bonds and $1,000 in cash, part of which they had inherited. The Woods were getting by in the sense that they managed to live from year to year, they ate reasonably well, and they were adequately sheltered. Yet there can be little doubt that they were poor according to any reasonable standards of living for this country.

The aged

One of the largest groups among the American poor is the aged. About two and a half million low-income families, living for the most part in large metropolitan areas, are headed by a person over sixty-five years of age. They are predominantly white.

Most of the aged poor are couples. There were two million of them in 1960. An additional half million were elderly women, largely widows living with their children.

As in the case of the farmers, the money incomes of the aged often fail to tell the whole story. Many older people have their homes paid for or are living on savings which do not show up in their current incomes. There are some elderly people whose income is only $1,000 a year but who manage to get to Florida every winter by drawing on their savings. These are undoubtedly the exceptions rather than the rule. Most of the aged depend on social security or other pensions. While these have gone up, they have not risen sufficiently to keep the incomes of the aged on a par with those of the rest of the population. Younger men can always take on a second job when they feel they are falling behind— and millions do. They also can send their wives out to work—and millions do that too. The aged have no such option and so they tend to fall behind in a booming economy. In view of this fact, it is surprising indeed that the aged have not increased as a proportion of the poor.

One of the striking facts revealed in any examination of the financial situation of the aged is the extent of their dependence on forms of income other than earnings. In 1960, about 36 percent of all families headed by a person sixty-five years old or over derived all of their income from social security payments, private pensions, and public assistance. About 60 percent of those with incomes under $3,000 did no paid work. These facts, of course, only confirm what nearly everyone knows: large numbers of older people do not work.

Families headed by persons over sixty-five are much smaller, on the average, than those headed by younger people. Their "needs" are also less, on the average. Therefore, a poverty line of $3,000 for them may seem unreasonable. An examination of the figures below suggests, however, that the total number included among the poor might not be changed greatly if an alternative definition of poverty had been used. About three-fourths of all aged families at all income levels were couples. About 60 percent of them had incomes under $3,000 in 1960. If $2,500 had been used as the poverty line, about 50 percent would have been included and even a $2,000 income limit would have included 36 percent. But there were also quite a few larger families headed by persons over sixty-five and for them even $3,000 as the poverty line may be unreasonably low. About 28 percent of the aged families with four persons had incomes under $3,000. A poverty line of $4,000 might have been more reasonable for this group and that would bring the proportion up to 33 percent. Similarly, about 30 percent of the aged families with five or more persons had incomes under $3,000. The proportion would have been raised to 38 percent had a poverty line of $4,000 been used.

A large proportion of the aged have very limited resources to fall back on in case of emergency. About 30 percent of all aged families have no liquid assets whatever and another 20 percent had less than $1,000 in 1960. Most of the assets of the aged are tied up in their homes or in life insurance rather than in forms that can be readily converted into cash in case of emergency.

Table v-4	*Income of families headed by a person aged 65 or over, in 1960*				
Income level	All families	Two persons	Three persons	Four persons	Five or more persons
Under $2,000	31%	36%	20%	18%	18%
Between $2,000 and $3,000	20	24	13	10	12
Between $3,000 and $4,000	12	12	16	6	8
$4,000 and over	36	29	52	67	62

U.S. Senate, Special Committee on Aging, *Background Facts on the Financing of Health Care of the Aged*, 87th Congress, 2nd Session, p. 36.

Broken families

The broken family, sometimes referred to as the fatherless home, is another major segment of the poor. There were one and a half million families like this in 1960, and virtually all concentrated in large metropolitan areas. About one million of these families were white and one-half million were nonwhite.

The large proportion of nonwhites within this group reflects the instability of family life among the Negroes. Every fifth Negro child is born out of wedlock and mothers of many of these children are left to fend for themselves in a hostile world. Even if they were accepted by society their economic lot would not be much better than it is because of their lack of skill or experience. Desertion, which is the poor man's divorce, may also be a greater cause of broken families among Negroes than among whites.

The women who head broken families are almost equally divided into three age groups: under thirty-five, thirty-five to forty-four, and forty-five to sixty-four. The half million or so who are over sixty-five were counted with the aged population.

Many of the problems that face the fatherless home were found in the home of Mrs. Scilaro and her family in Philadelphia, when her case was reported to the Joint Economic Committee in 1950. Mrs. Scilaro was born in Italy and came to this country to marry her husband. She could neither read nor write. She had seven children, two of whom died. The five children living with her in 1950 ranged from twelve to seventeen. Her husband died shortly after the birth of her youngest child.

Upon the death of her husband, full responsibility for the support of the family fell on Mrs. Scilaro's shoul-

75

ders. She went to work in a garment factory as a seam-stress; her take-home pay was $30 a week or about $1,500 in 1950. Her oldest son quit school at seventeen and went to work in a restaurant, where he earned $5 a week plus some of his meals. He was promised a better job as soon as he turned eighteen. The other Scilaro children also planned to quit school when they reached seventeen.

The Scilaros lived in a little house on a very narrow street in the old part of Philadelphia. On the first floor were a living room and a tiny kitchen. Winding stairs led to three small bedrooms on the second floor. There was running cold water in the kitchen but no other plumb-ing. The toilet was outside in the back yard. A single coal stove in the kitchen supplied heat for the whole house in the winter. The kitchen also had a gas cook stove and an electric refrigerator that was purchased for $50. Mrs. Scilaro paid for it at the rate of $1 a week.

The family was constantly in debt. All purchases were made in neighborhood stores on credit and the bills were paid whenever Mrs. Scilaro could pay them. Very little clothing was purchased and that largely from a secondhand clothing store in the neighborhood. The only saving grace for this family was that they were all basically healthy and there were no medical bills.

The family was very close-knit. The boys all played together and refused to separate to play with others of their own age. Occasionally they would earn money shining shoes and would go to the movies together. Most of their time was spent playing on their own narrow street.

Nonwhite families

In 1960 there were about one million nonwhite fam-ilies (over 90 percent Negroes) living in or near large cities and headed by a man under sixty-five years old. Much has been written and said about the plight of the Negro. Their overrepresentation among the poor should surprise no one. There are undoubtedly many factors that keep the Negro at the bottom, but there can be little doubt that racial discrimination is a key cause.

In 1962, President Kennedy's Council of Economic Advisers prepared an estimate of the economic loss to the United States resulting from racial discrimination in employment. This study showed that if the education and training of the Negro population were fully utilized by the elimination of racial barriers in employment, our national product might rise by as much as 2½ percent each year. In 1961, this would have increased our income as a nation by $13 billion. These wasted skills amounted to one-fourth of the total that was spent for national defense in that year. The monetary loss in national income is, of course, only a small part of the total social burden of discrimination. When the costs of higher crime rates, poor health, urban decay, and many other problems that stem directly or indirectly from discrimination are added, the amount becomes astronomical.

An examination of the jobs held by heads of non-white poor families makes obvious the reason for their poverty. One-fourth of them are laborers and an additional third work as domestics or in the service trades. About three out of every five of these family heads work in these three low-paying occupations. When the semi-skilled factory workers are added, about 85 percent of the nonwhite poor families are accounted for.

Other groups among the poor

Finally, there is the fifth group, whose poverty has no apparent explanation in census statistics—white families living in or near large cities and headed by a man in his productive years. What are these three million families like? Explanations based on personal or environmental factors could be made for the farm poor, the aged poor, the widowed and divorced poor, and the Negro poor. What is there to say about the white poor?

First of all it must be recognized that these three million families come from a total of thirty million who have the same characteristics—that is, they are white, live in the city, and are headed by a man under sixty-five. In the normal course of events, some of these families would be expected to be poor. Some of the men heading these families are bound to be ill or disabled and the families suffer as a result. Others may lack the intelligence to learn a trade or to hold down a responsible job. As a result they are cast into the most menial and lowest paying occupations. Still others get bad "breaks." Their employer goes out of business or has a bad year and their incomes suffer as a result.

The diversity of this group is reflected in the kinds of work they do. The heads of nonwhite poor families were very highly concentrated in the labor, service, and semiskilled factory trades; about 85 percent of them were employed in these occupations. Only one-half of the white poor family heads worked in these occupations. An additional 20 percent were craftsmen and 30 percent were white-collar professional or managerial workers. Some of those in the better-paying occupations may have just been starting out on their careers and could look forward to higher incomes in the future. Nearly half of the total were over forty-five, and while they were still too young for the "scrap heap," they may have had difficulty in getting good jobs because of their "advanced age."

Many different kinds of families are included in this

group. For some, like the Duncans of Portland, Oregon, and the Mahoneys of Pittsburgh, poverty is only temporary. In 1950, when Mr. Duncan was interviewed for the Joint Economic Committee, he was twenty-nine years old and was working as an auto repairman. His income was only $2,000, but he had just started working at his trade. Frank Mahoney and his wife were in much the same position. Their income in 1950 was $1,900, but Mr. Mahoney was only twenty-eight years old and was working for his master's degree under the G.I. Bill. They would not be poor for long.

For others equally young, however, the future prospects were not so good. Frank Petrov, age twenty-five, his wife Maria, age twenty, and their four-year-old son also lived in Pittsburgh. In 1950, when this case was reported, Mr. Petrov was working as a messenger for a telegraph company. His earnings were $1,500. This employment climaxed a long line of poor jobs. He quit school in the seventh grade and was in the service during World War II, but was discharged because of poor health. After his discharge he went to work in a steel mill, but he quit this job because he was too nervous to stand the work. He then went to work in a pants factory, where he earned $18 a week. About this time he met his wife, who was employed in a suitcase factory and also earned $18 a week. Shortly after their marriage, Mrs. Petrov became pregnant and had to leave her job.

Maria's background is not too different from her husband's. She is one of ten children of Italian immigrants. She also quit school in the seventh grade, when she was fifteen years old. She was sixteen when she married Frank. Despite their poverty and uncertain future, both parents were very anxious to have more children. The social worker reported that when the inadvisability of increasing their family was mentioned Maria replied,

"Whether you can afford children or not, you sometimes just decide to have them."

Frank and Maria were both in poor health. Maria suffered from indigestion, obesity, and other ailments which required regular treatment at a public clinic. Frank was nervous. He could not do physical work. His wife reported that if anything disturbed him, such as a reprimand for taking too long to deliver a telegram, he would come home and kick the furniture, sometimes breaking it.

The family moved very often, a total of ten times during five years of marriage. At the time of the interview, they were living in a public housing project which they regarded as the best home they had ever had. The home was well kept and neatly furnished with second-hand pieces. The most valued possession was the television set.

The financial prospects for this family were clearly not good. Uneducated, unskilled, and in poor health, Frank could hardly expect ever to move out of the ranks of the poor. The tensions caused by financial pressures would undoubtedly increase in time as children came and bills mounted. But the pleasures were bound to increase too. They had a large, close-knit family and many friends. There would be poverty; but there would also be parties, evenings spent in loud discussion, weddings, picnics, and all the other pleasures that make life bearable for some of the poor.

Summary

Poverty is nothing to joke about. It is real, serious, and important. But it is also one of those emotionally charged words that can trap you if you are not careful.

Much needless soul searching can be avoided if it is recognized at the outset that there is no objective definition of poverty any more than there is an objective definition of art or beauty. The standards of poverty are established by society. They can be arbitrarily defined for a given time and place; but they vary from place to place and they differ from time to time for a given place. Professor Dorothy Brady, who has devoted a lifetime to this field of study, once wrote: "When faced directly with the problem of determining [poverty] for a given time and place, the theorist will deny the possibility of a unique answer and the propagandist will settle for one of many solutions if the result suits his purposes." The prophetic wisdom of this remark is most clear when you see the way in which politicians and propagandists manipulate income figures to meet their particular needs.

Many people refuse to recognize a simple statistical fact. If a distribution has a middle and a top it must also have a bottom and somebody must be there. The important question is why they are there and how much they get. People are not all equally endowed with good health, intelligence, creativity, drive, etc. In any society a premium will be paid to those who are most productive.

The individual can legitimately demand from a democratic society that he be given the chance to develop his God-given talents. Society, in turn, must place a floor beneath those who fall to the bottom so as to minimize their suffering.

On the first point, there is still a long way to go in America. There is still much evidence of discrimination, neglected talent, and the transmission of poverty from one generation to the next. The picture is, of course, not all black. Millions of immigrants who came to this country with only the clothes on their backs have lived to see their children outgrow the filthy slums of the Lower East

Side, Hell's Kitchen, and other choice spots that match the worst you would find today. But there is still a long road ahead, particularly for the Negroes, Puerto Ricans, and other minorities.

On the second point, there is much to be proud of in the United States. As previously stated, in 1929 about half of the families and individuals had incomes below $3,000 (in 1962 dollars). That number has been more than cut in half. At the current rate of progress perhaps only about 10 percent of the population will be below this poverty line in 1980.

Does this mean that poverty will be virtually eliminated in the next fifteen years? The historical evidence points strongly against such a conclusion. The chances are that our standards will be lifted a little higher, our belts will be opened another notch, and there will still be a large block of families living under new and higher substandard conditions.

The Bureau of Labor Statistics has estimated that the cost of a "modest but adequate" level of living (excluding taxes) for a working-class family of four persons in New York City was about $4,000 in 1947 and about $5,200 in 1959 (both figures in terms of 1961 purchasing power). In other words, the "modest but adequate" level of living rose by 28 percent in New York City in this twelve-year period. At this rate of growth, a working-class family living in New York City will be considered poor in 1975 if its income is under $7,000 (in 1961 dollars). Even families making considerably more than this will be considered poor if allowance is made for normal inflation and taxes.

Do these numbers seem unreasonably high? Well, they are no more unreasonable than the present standard of living seemed a few years ago. How far this nation has come from that bleak day in January, 1937, when

President Roosevelt stated in his second inaugural address: "I see millions of families trying to live on incomes so meager that the pall of family disaster hangs over them day by day." There still are families like that, to be sure. There always will be. But abject poverty of this type is dwindling. When you speak of the millions of poor today, you mean something entirely different.

CHAPTER VI

Race, creed, and color— the income of minorities

The Negro

"One hundred years of delay have passed since President Lincoln freed the slaves, yet their heirs, their grandsons are not fully free. They are not yet freed from the bonds of injustice. They are not yet freed from social and economic oppression." These are not the remarks of a rabble rouser or a soap-box orator. They were made by the President of the United States in a nationwide address on June 12, 1963—the eve of the admission of two Negro youths to the University of Alabama.

All figures collected in the census—on housing, education, occupation, income—show that the Negro still ranks among the poorest of the poor. His lowly position has been documented so many times and in so many ways that presenting the evidence seems like proving the obvious. Yet what is obvious to some is not even apparent to others. Facts form the only solid basis for the discussion out of which justice and truth may emerge. Though "redress is being sought in the streets, in demonstrations, parades, and protests," it is not yet too late for facts.

There is a general impression that the Negro has largely left the South. This is not the case. In 1960 there were 18.9 million Negroes in the United States. About 11.3 million, or 60 percent, lived in the South, 3 million lived in the Northeast, 3.5 million lived in the North Central states, and only 1 million lived in the West. Within the South, a large proportion of the Negroes have migrated to urban areas. Three major concentrations of Negroes can be identified in the United States. About one-third live in southern cities, about one-fourth live on southern farms, and the remainder live in the North and West.

The income they receive

Income is one of the best measures of economic status. By this standard, the position of Negroes is quite low in comparison with whites in most states. More disturbing is this sad fact: in many states their situation relative to the whites has grown *worse*, not better. The income gap between the races generally widened during the fifties. Shown below is a comparison of the median income of white and Negro males by state for 1949 and 1959. The figures are restricted to states with 100,000 or more Negroes.

The income position of Negroes relative to whites is most favorable in the North and in California. In most northern states, except New Jersey, the average income of Negroes was about 70 percent or more of the white average in 1959. The situation for Negroes was best in states such as Michigan, Pennsylvania, and Indiana, where unionized heavy industries are concentrated. In these states, the median income of Negroes was about three-fourths of that received by whites.

Negroes do not do as well in the South as in the North. In the District of Columbia, the average for Negroes was 72 percent of the white average, about the same as in many northern states. This relatively high ratio is due partly to the influence of the federal government, which is the major employer in the District of Columbia. It also reflects the fact that many of the higher paid federal employees—who are white—live in the suburban areas outside the District and are not counted in the comparisons with Negroes living within it.

Except for the District of Columbia, which most

Table VI-1   *The income gap—regional differences in the incomes of white and Negro males in 1949 and 1959*

(For states with 100,00 or more Negroes in 1960)

State	1949			1959		
	White	Negro		White	Negro	
		Amount	Percent of white		Amount	Percent of white
United States overall	$2,582	$1,356	53%	$4,337	$2,254	52%
Northeast						
Massachusetts	2,630	1,944	74	4,452	3,063	69
Connecticut	2,809	2,023	72	5,033	3,545	70
New York	2,929	2,097	72	4,812	3,372	70
New Jersey	3,033	1,977	65	5,172	3,375	65
Pennsylvania	2,638	2,073	79	4,369	3,246	74
North Central						
Ohio	2,852	2,146	75	4,903	3,492	71
Indiana	2,696	2,211	82	4,483	3,520	79
Illinois	3,030	2,260	75	5,056	3,651	72
Michigan	3,039	2,659	87	4,983	3,768	76
Missouri	2,224	1,611	72	3,863	2,616	68

Table vi-i (*Cont.*)

State	1949			1959		
	White	Negro		White	Negro	
		Amount	Percent of white		Amount	Percent of white
South						
Maryland	2,782	1,601	58	4,880	2,769	57
District of Columbia	3,242	2,182	67	4,694	3,376	72
Virginia	2,255	1,220	54	3,758	1,907	51
North Carolina	1,872	1,002	54	3,040	1,318	43
South Carolina	2,043	801	39	3,224	1,140	35
Georgia	1,870	919	49	3,420	1,510	44
Florida	2,239	1,185	53	3,769	2,080	55
Kentucky	1,701	1,197	70	2,938	1,787	61
Tennessee	1,685	1,141	68	2,939	1,637	56
Alabama	1,809	957	53	3,409	1,446	42
Mississippi	1,462	605	41	2,796	904	32
Arkansas	1,423	759	53	2,553	990	39
Louisiana	2,228	997	45	4,001	1,609	40
Oklahoma	2,041	992	49	3,489	1,704	49
Texas	2,272	1,202	53	3,756	1,916	51
West						
California	2,966	2,121	72	5,109	3,553	70

U.S. *Census of Population: 1960, Detailed Characteristics,*
Table 133; and U.S. *Census of Population: 1950,* Vol. II,
Table 87.

Southerners do not regard as the South, Kentucky was
the only southern state in which the average income of
Negroes reached 60 percent of the white average. In
some states of the old Confederacy—Virginia, Florida,
Tennessee, and Texas—the Negro average was about

half of the white average. In the deep South, the Negro average was well under half the white average, dropping to as low as one-third in Mississippi and South Carolina.

Out of a total of twenty-six states (including the District of Columbia) for which data are shown, the ratio of Negro to white income increased slightly between 1949 and 1959 in two states (District of Columbia and Florida) and it was unchanged in two others (New Jersey and Oklahoma). In every other state there was a widening of the gap between the incomes of whites and Negroes and in some cases it was fairly substantial. In Michigan, for example, the ratio of average Negro income to white income dropped from 87 percent in 1949 to 76 percent in 1959. In several southern states, notably Kentucky, Tennessee, Alabama, and Mississippi, there was also a marked reduction in the relative income position of Negroes.

How they live

The low income of the Negro shows up very clearly in the kind of housing he has. A very large proportion of Negro children are reared in homes that are inadequate by modern standards. The situation is better than it was ten years ago, but it is still poor in many parts of the country. The figures below tell the story better than words.

For the country as a whole, nearly half of the non-white families live in homes that are either already so run down that they are hazardous to live in or are badly in need of repair. Between 1950 and 1960 the proportion living in dilapidated housing was cut in half; but much of the change seems to have been a shift from dilapidated to deteriorating homes. Even in 1960 only

Table VI-2   *Nonwhite housing conditions in 1960 and 1950, by region*

Year and condition of housing	United States	South	North and West
1960			
Sound			
With all plumbing facilities	43%	30%	58%
Lacking plumbing facilities	11	15	7
Deteriorating	29	32	25
Dilapidated	17	23	10
1950			
Not dilapidated			
With all plumbing facilities	28%	13%	53%
Lacking plumbing facilities	39	47	26
Dilapidated	33	39	21

U.S. Bureau of the Census Press Release, March 23, 1961.

two nonwhite families out of every five lived in sound structures with hot and cold running water, a bath or shower, and a flush toilet.

Housing conditions for nonwhites are worse in the South than in the rest of the country. In 1950, only 13 percent of the nonwhite families lived in sound structures with all facilities. Despite vast improvements, only 30 percent of the nonwhites in the South had this kind of a home in 1960. The proportion was about twice as great in the North and West. Over half of the nonwhite families in the South continue to live in dilapidated or deteriorating structures.

Employment and earnings

The price that Negroes pay for their dark skins is nowhere more obvious than in employment. In almost every group of jobs they earn less money than whites because they hold the lowest paying jobs in that group. They are clerks instead of managers, laborers instead of bricklayers, machine operators instead of toolmakers. But that is only part of their disadvantage. They often get lower pay even when doing exactly the same work as whites. White men earn more simply because they are white, regardless of the job. The details of facts and figures paint this pathetic picture in stark detail.

About 3,600,000 Negro men were employed in April, 1960. One million worked as laborers; an additional half million were employed in the service trades as janitors, porters, cooks, elevator operators, and the like. Together, these two very low-paying occupation groups accounted for about 40 percent of all jobs held by Negro men. Even within these low-paying jobs, Negroes earned far less than whites. Among farm laborers, whites averaged 35 percent more than nonwhites; the medians were $1,300 and $800 respectively. Among nonfarm laborers the differential was 25 percent in favor of the whites (the average was $3,200 for whites and $2,400 for nonwhites); and among service workers average earnings for whites was 29 percent higher ($3,600 as compared with $2,500). Not all service workers are low-paid. Within this occupation group, average earnings for Negroes range from about $4,300 for policemen and firemen to about $2,500 for janitors and porters. Only about 4 percent of the firemen and policemen were Negro; 37 percent of the janitors were.

A large proportion of Negro men work as factory

hands or in other semiskilled jobs ranging all the way from parking lot attendants to truck drivers. About one-fourth of the total fall in this occupation group. Earnings there are somewhat higher than in the service trades, averaging about $3,000 in 1959; but still the Negroes made about 32 percent less than the whites, who averaged $4,400. The main reason for the lower than average earnings of nonwhite workers within this broad occupation group is their concentration in its lower paid jobs, and very often in its lower paying industries. For example, about one-fourth of all semiskilled Negroes are truck drivers or deliverymen. Whites in this occupation averaged $4,500, nonwhites only $2,600, a differential of about 42 percent. The difference is probably due to the fact that most nonwhites in this occupation work as lower paid deliverymen rather than as truck drivers. Relatively large numbers of semiskilled Negroes also work at such low-paying jobs as parking lot attendants, packers and wrappers, laundry and dry-cleaning workers, and taxi drivers and chauffeurs. About one-third of all men employed by laundry and dry-cleaning plants were Negro. Their earnings averaged only $2,600, about the same as janitors and porters. This fact is significant and disheartening. Even when Negroes succeed in "getting ahead in the world" and become truck drivers and semi-skilled factory workers, who have higher status than janitors and porters, their earnings do not increase appreciably, and in some cases not at all.

Only about 10 percent of the Negro men worked as craftsmen. Their average earnings were $3,500 as compared with $5,300 for whites, a differential of about 35 percent. Negro craftsmen were about equally divided into three occupational categories: construction workers, mechanics, and all others. Their average earnings in construction was $2,900, only about $400 more than the average earned by janitors or porters. In contrast, white craftsmen in the construction trades averaged about $4,800. Among mechanics, whites averaged $4,800, non-whites, $3,500.

Within the white-collar fields, relatively few Negroes are employed as managerial or sales workers. In 1960 there were a total of 31,000 salaried managers who were Negro, 32,000 owners of unincorporated businesses (small retail stores for the most part), and 47,000 salesmen. Salaried managers who were Negro averaged $4,400, 37 percent below the $7,000 received by whites. Negro businessmen averaged only $3,300, or about 43 percent below the white average. The average income received by Negro salesmen ($2,800) was about 44 percent below the white average and only several hundred dollars more than that of porters and janitors.

Clerical work is a major source of white-collar employment for Negro men, and their earnings in this occupation compare more favorably with those of whites than in most other occupations. About 179,000 Negro men were employed as clerical workers in 1960 and their average earnings ($4,100) was only 16 percent below the white average. One reason for the relatively small differential is that a large proportion of Negro clerical workers are employed by the U.S. Post Office, where their average earnings do not differ appreciably from those received by whites.

Professional and technical work, the highest paid of all, was relatively unimportant among Negroes and it paid them substantially less than it did whites. A total of about 113,000 Negro men had professional and technical employment in April, 1960. The two largest categories were schoolteachers and clergymen, who accounted for about 40 percent of the group. Partly because of their heavy concentration in these two relatively low-paying professions, their earnings averaged only $4,600, about 32 percent below the white average of $6,700.

Like the men, Negro women are highly concentrated in low-paying jobs. Unlike the men, however, the earnings differential between the races was not appreciable in most occupations.

Nearly 900,000 Negro women, or over one-third of

Table VI-3 *Jobs and pay of Negro men in 1960*

Occupation *	Number of Negro workers	Percent of occupation that is Negro	Median earnings White	Median earnings Non-white
Negro men employed	3,644,000	8.4%	$4,855	$2,703
Professional and technical				
workers	113,000	2.5	6,693	4,563
Engineers	4,000	0.5	7,452	7,076
Medical and other				
health workers	12,000	3.4	7,953	4,642
Schoolteachers	28,000	6.8	5,701	4,450
Farmers and farm managers	154,000	6.5	2,324	788
Managers, officials, and				
proprietors	63,000	1.4	6,719	3,869
Salaried	31,000	1.0	7,025	4,433
Self-employed	32,000	1.9	5,831	3,318
Clerical workers	179,000	5.9	4,848	4,072
Mail carriers	20,000	10.4	5,309	5,101
Sales workers	47,000	1.6	5,036	2,809
Craftsmen and foremen	357,000	4.2	5,316	3,480
Construction craftsmen	120,000	5.5	4,839	2,855
Foremen	16,000	1.5	6,651	4,791
Mechanics and repair-				
men	117,000	5.3	4,798	3,478

* This table does not include all occupations.

Table VI-3 (Cont.)

Occupation	Number of Negro workers	Percent of occupation that is Negro	Median earnings White	Non-white
Semiskilled workers	887,000	10.3	4,445	3,040
Trucking	248,000	12.7	4,539	2,638
Laundry and dry cleaning	36,000	33.3	3,253	2,600
Durable goods manufacturing	147,000	9.8	4,695	3,749
Nondurable goods manufacturing	114,000	9.1	4,465	3,272
Nonmanufacturing industries	77,000	14.6	4,496	2,859
Private household workers	27,000	44.7	956	1,216
Service workers	508,000	19.5	3,582	2,529
Janitors	265,000	37.2	2,833	2,543
Police and firemen	25,000	3.8	4,932	4,276
Waiters, cooks, and bartenders	81,000	15.8	3,267	2,759
Farm laborers	257,000	21.4	1,256	816
Nonfarm laborers	745,000	24.9	3,210	2,394

U.S. Census of Population: 1960, Detailed Characteristics, United States Summary, Tables 205 and 208.

the total employed in April, 1960, were private household workers, a dignified title for women who clean other women's homes. These women averaged only $700 in earnings in 1959, about the same as the average for white women in this occupation. The average annual figure is very low partly because household workers, even more than other women, so often have part-time jobs.

The second major source of employment for Negro women was the service trades. Over 500,000 women, or about one-fifth of the total who were employed in April, 1960, worked as waitresses, cooks, charwomen, hospital attendants, and practical nurses. The average earnings of nonwhite women in this occupation was $1,400, the same as that received by white women in the service trades.

Factory work was a third major source of employment for Negro women. About 310,000 engaged in semi-skilled jobs in April, 1960. Somewhat more than half of these women worked in manufacturing plants, but about 100,000 worked in low-paying laundry and dry-cleaning plants. It was partly for this reason that their overall average earnings was only $1,800 in 1959, or about 23 percent below the white average of $2,400. Nonwhite women who worked in durable-goods manufacturing plants made an average of $2,500 as compared with $2,900 for white women; nonwhite women employed in soft-goods factories averaged $2,000 as compared with $2,300 for white women.

Relatively few Negro women had white-collar employment in April, 1960. About 180,000, less than 10 percent of the total, were clerical workers. About 50,000 were secretaries and typists, while most of the others did general clerical work. The average earnings of nonwhite women who were clerical workers was $3,000 in 1959, about the same as that received by white women in this occupation.

The number of professional and technical workers among Negro women was about the same as the number of clerical workers, 175,000. About 100,000 were schoolteachers and more than 30,000 were professional nurses. These two occupations accounted for 75 percent of all Negro women employed in professional and technical jobs. The average earnings of nonwhite professional women was $3,600, the same as that received by white women.

Table VI-4   *Jobs and pay of Negro women in 1960*

Occupation *	Number of Negro workers	Percent of occupation that is Negro	Median earnings	
			White	Non-white
Negro women employed	2,455,000	11.6%	$2,393	$1,219
Professional and technical workers	175,000	6.4	3,641	3,571
Medical and other health workers	44,000	5.7	3,126	3,057
Schoolteachers	94,000	8.5	4,161	3,790
Clerical workers	182,000	2.9	3,018	2,993
Secretaries, stenographers and typists	52,000	2.4	3,241	3,231
Sales workers	36,000	2.2	1,496	1,562
Semiskilled workers	310,000	9.5	2,371	1,829
Laundry and dry cleaning	99,000	35.9	1,667	1,542
Durable goods manufacturing	27,000	6.9	2,948	2,549
Nondurable goods manufacturing	76,000	9.1	2,346	1,964
Nonmanufacturing industries	18,000	17.9	2,001	1,440
Private household workers	888,000	53.4	661	704
Service workers	520,000	18.3	1,391	1,365
Charwomen	51,000	25.0	1,325	1,354
Practical nurses	32,000	16.3	1,805	2,031
Waitresses and cooks	135,000	11.2	1,148	1,158

* This table does not include all occupations.

U.S. *Census of Population: 1960, Detailed Characteristics, United States Summary,* Tables 205 and 208.

Private household workers 888,000									
Clerical workers 182,000									
Waitresses 135,000									
Teachers 94,000									
Saleswomen 36,000									

1960
Average pay of women all jobs

nonwhite	white
$1,219	$2,393

Percent of occupation that is Negro	53.4%	2.9%	11.2%	8.5%	2.2%

median earnings

nonwhite	white	nonwhite	white	nonwhite	white	nonwhite	white	nonwhite	white
$704	$661	$2,993	$3,018	$1,158	$1,148	$3,790	$4,161	$1,562	$1,496

Jobs and pay of Negro Women

Is the Negroes' lot improving?

The above figures document the shocking facts of American economic life. Though the shackles of slavery have been removed and the whip of the taskmaster has been broken, their effect remains and the Negro exists on the crumbs of U.S. affluence. With few exceptions he cannot get a well-paying job.

There is a general impression that this situation has improved in recent years. Senator Jacob Javits of New York, for example, states in his book, *Discrimination U.S.A.:* "The tremendous progress of the last three decades in increasing equality of opportunity of employment must be credited to the influence of the federal government, to FEPC legislation, to the labor unions, and

97

to civic and community relations organizations. This is dramatically shown by the gains scored for the Negro worker, the chief victim of discrimination." The Department of Labor reports that "occupational differences between Negroes and whites are still large, but Negroes have raised their occupational levels appreciably faster, in the past 22 years, than whites." This conclusion is valid as a generalization for the country as a whole. However, most of the improvement in the occupational status of the Negro since 1940 has been due to his movement from the rural South to the urban industrial areas rather than to any major improvement in job opportunities. The problem can be seen more clearly, perhaps, in the following perspective.

There has been a general upgrading of occupational skills for both whites and Negroes as the American economy has moved away from agriculture and become more complex and industrialized. As a result, Negroes who were once highly concentrated in sharecropping and farm labor have now moved up to unskilled and semi-skilled factory jobs; some have moved into white-collar employment. But there has been a parallel upgrading of jobs held by whites. The real question is whether the relative upward movement has been faster for nonwhites than for whites. The answer, based on statistical tests (see page 99) that have been applied to the data collected in the past three censuses, seems to be no. Although the occupational status of nonwhites relative to whites has improved for the country as a whole, in most states the nonwhite male now has about the same occupational distribution relative to the whites that he had in 1940 and 1950. The results, summarized in Table VI-5, show that there have been few significant changes in the occupational distribution of nonwhite males relative to whites during the past twenty years.

Computation of occupational index

This index is based on a standardization procedure which attempts to show in a single summary measure how white and nonwhite employment would compare if all workers in a given occupation received the same earnings and the only difference among them was their percent distribution by occupation. In other words, the average earnings of an occupation is used as a weight; the higher paid the occupation, the greater the weight assigned to it. The operation of the procedure can be demonstrated in a simple numerical example. Assume that all workers can be classified into three types: laborers with average earnings of $1,000; semiskilled operatives who average $2,000; and craftsmen who average $3,000. Suppose further that we have 100 white workers distributed as follows: 20 laborers, 30 operatives, and 50 craftsmen; and that we have 100 nonwhite workers 50 of whom are laborers, 30 operatives, and 20 craftsmen. It is possible from this information to develop an index that would permit a quantitative comparison of white and nonwhite employment. The calculations are shown here.

White	Nonwhite
Laborers 20 × 1,000 = 20,000	50 × 1,000 = 50,000
Operatives 30 × 2,000 = 60,000	30 × 2,000 = 60,000
Craftsmen 50 × 3,000 = 150,000	20 × 3,000 = 60,000
230,000	170,000
White index = $\dfrac{230,000}{6,000} = 38$	Non-white index = $\dfrac{170,000}{6,000} = 28$

On the basis of the information given, whites had an index of 38 and nonwhites had an index of only 28. Whites, therefore, had a higher occupational index. Of course, this was known to start with because 50 percent of the whites were craftsmen as compared with only 20 percent of the nonwhites; but without a standardization procedure there was no simple way to summarize this information so as to include all occupations.

Table VI-5   *Occupational index by states: ratio of nonwhite to white men in 1940, 1950, and 1960*

(For states with 100,000 or more Negroes in 1960. See text for explanation of occupational index.)

States	1940	1950	1960
United States	.70	.77	.81
Northeast			
Massachusetts	.81	.84	.88
Connecticut	.82	.84	.83
New York	.85	.86	.87
New Jersey	.78	.80	.83
Pennsylvania	.85	.85	.86
North Central			
Ohio	.87	.86	.86
Indiana	.92	.90	.89
Illinois	.89	.88	.88
Michigan	.91	.90	.88
Missouri	.87	.88	.86
South			
Maryland	.71	.75	.78
District of Columbia	.75	.77	.79

Table vi-5 (*Cont.*)

States	1940	1950	1960
Virginia	.73	.76	.76
North Carolina	.71	.72	.73
South Carolina	.62	.65	.69
Georgia	.71	.73	.73
Florida	.68	.67	.69
Kentucky	.93	.89	.83
Tennessee	.84	.83	.79
Alabama	.75	.77	.74
Mississippi	.63	.66	.64
Arkansas	.73	.74	.77
Louisiana	.66	.70	.74
Oklahoma	.77	.78	.82
Texas	.73	.77	.79
West			
California	.70	.78	.84

U.S. Senate, 88th Congress, 1st Session, *Hearings Before the Committee on Labor and Public Welfare on Bills Relating to Equal Employment Opportunities*, July and August, 1963, p. 323.

This standardization procedure, using actual figures instead of the assumed figures in the above description, was applied to ten major occupation groups. The weights used were the median earnings for males in each occupation group in 1959. White and nonwhite indexes for males were constructed for each state with 100,000 or more Negroes in 1960. The indexes were computed for 1940, 1950, and 1960. For each state, the nonwhite index was expressed as a ratio of the white index. In the illustration used above, the ratio would be .74, which is obtained by dividing 28 by 38. This ratio is shown in Table vi-5 for each state for 1940, 1950, and 1960.

Another current fallacy is the belief that Negroes find full employment opportunities in government service. The concentration of Negroes in the lower paid jobs that was so evident in the figures for the country as a whole also appears in the federal employment statistics shown below. Not only are Negroes disproportionately represented in the lower-paid manual and clerical federal jobs, but they are barely represented at all in the middle and upper echelons of government service.

Many of the very top jobs are appointive and so the virtual absence of Negroes from these positions could be attributed to discrimination. But there are few Negroes even in the middle administrative and professional federal jobs, almost all of which are in the regular Civil Service.

Most of these jobs are filled by people who come into the Civil Service at lower positions and move up through the ranks. It is undoubtedly true that many Negroes are not recommended for promotion because their supervisors are prejudiced against them. And yet it would be easy to exaggerate the importance of this argument. There are some federal agencies that have for years conducted intensive campaigns to find, train, and promote Negroes who show the capacity to move to better paid jobs. These programs have been successful for the most part in ferreting out talents that might otherwise have been lost; yet even in these agencies the Negroes represent a very small proportion of the higher paid employees. The reason in these cases is not discrimination but a lack of people with education, training, and aptitude to move up the line.

The Library of Congress is a case in point. Librarian Quincy Mumford is justifiably proud of his agency's record on equal employment opportunity. He told Con-

1962			
Negro employees	66,101	29,204	1,406
Percent of grade that is Negro	18.2%	5.5%	0.8%

Jobs and pay of Negro government employees

Table vi-6. Report Issued by President's Committee on Equal Employment Opportunity, May 24, 1963.

gress, "Job opportunities are open at all times to Negroes in the Library in accordance with their qualifications. It is our policy not to tolerate any discrimination in respect to race or creed or otherwise. We have had a non-discrimination program for a long time." Nevertheless, the facts show that in Grades 1–4, the library staff is 36 percent Negro, in Grades 5–11 it is 13 percent Negro, and in Grades 12 and above it is only 0.8 percent Negro. The very low proportion of Negroes in the top-grade jobs is attributed by Mumford to "the minimum of qualified Negro applicants."

The problem is obviously complicated. Both prejudice and a shortage of trained people are undoubtedly

8%
of
Whites

15%
of
Non-
Whites

16%
of
Puerto
Ricans

14%
of
Whites

29%
of
Non-
Whites

37%
of
Puerto
Ricans

under
$2,000

$2,000
to
$4,000

Income of White, Nonwhite, and Puerto Rican
families in New York City: 1959

involved, and a solution will be found only by working on both fronts.

Puerto Ricans

Puerto Ricans represent one of the newer minority groups in the United States. There were about 856,000 Puerto Ricans living in this country at the time of the last census. Nearly three out of every four lived in New

Table VI-7. *U.S. Censuses of Population and Housing: 1960*, Census Tract Report for New York City.

York City, for the most part in Manhattan, the Bronx, and Brooklyn. It is reasonable to turn to the census results for New York City for a cross section of their economic status.

Income

The Department of Labor estimated in 1959 that a family of four living in New York City and its suburbs needed an income of about $6,000 to maintain a "modest but adequate" level of living. (This figure includes taxes and therefore differs from the one cited in Chapter 5.) About 60 percent of the Puerto Rican families in New York City have four or more persons. How many achieve this $6,000 figure?

Half the Puerto Rican families in New York City had incomes under $3,800 in 1959. The median for non-whites (99 percent Negro) in the city was $4,400, $600 greater, while the median for whites was $6,400. Four out of every five Puerto Rican families had incomes under $6,000 in 1959 (see pictograph [Table vi-7]). Keeping in mind the fact that many of these families are quite large and that they pay exorbitant rents for substandard homes, you can begin to appreciate their plight.

Education

Without education the opportunity to rise above the lowest levels is slim indeed. Perhaps because many Puerto Ricans are recent immigrants to this country, their educational attainment is far below that of the whites and even below that of Negroes in New York City. The average Puerto Rican in the city had only 7½ years of schooling as compared with 9½ years for Negroes and nearly 10½ years for whites. One out of every two adult Puerto Ricans in New York City had not gone beyond the seventh grade and nearly three out of every four had no formal education beyond the eighth grade. What chance do people with this little schooling have to make a decent living in a society where one-third of the salesmen and one-fourth of the office clerks have college training? You can see the transmission belt of poverty operating at full steam. The children will suffer because there is generally a very close association between an individual's own educational attainment and his plans to educate his children.

Housing

The poverty of Puerto Rican families in New York City is reflected in the poor quality of their housing. Only 60 percent of the Puerto Ricans in New York live in sound units, whereas 40 percent live in units that are either deteriorating or dilapidated. Evidently Puerto Ricans who live in the Bronx have higher economic status than those who live in Manhattan or Brooklyn. This pattern is reminiscent of that followed by the Jewish immigrants to New York in the early part of this century. The first sign of having "arrived" in the new world was a move away from the Lower East Side to the Bronx.

Table vi-8	Puerto Rican housing conditions in New York City: 1960			
Condition of housing	All of New York City	Man- hattan	Brooklyn	The Bronx
Sound	60%	52%	55%	72%
Deteriorating	30	35	33	22
Dilapidated	10	13	13	6

U.S. Censuses of Population and Housing: 1960, Census Tract Report for New York City.

The higher economic status of Bronx residents is reflected in the figures on educational attainment and family income. Median years of school completed was about one-half year greater in the Bronx (8.0) than in Manhattan. Moreover, family incomes were also somewhat higher in that borough. One-half of the Puerto Rican families in the Bronx had incomes over $4,100 in 1959. The median in Brooklyn was $300 lower ($3,900) and in Manhattan it was $600 lower ($3,500).

You might think there would be a substantial rent differential for the inferior housing, but that was not the case at all. The average rent paid by all Puerto Rican families in the city was $62 a month. Those living in sound units paid $64. In deteriorating units the average monthly rent was $59 and in dilapidated units it was $56. In each case, this rental amounted to about one-fifth of the annual income received by the average family. However, one Puerto Rican family out of every five in the city paid a third of their income for rent; in a large proportion of the cases it was rent for a substandard unit.

In New York City, Puerto Rican housing is inferior to that of nonwhites. Both are far inferior to that of whites. Indeed, Negroes and Puerto Ricans occupy about one-half of all the dilapidated units in the city even though they account for only about one-fifth of all households.

Has there been any improvement since 1950 in the economic status of Puerto Ricans relative to nonwhites (Negroes) in New York City? The tentative answer is "No."

According to the census results, the Negro has increased his schooling by one full year on the average, whereas there was a drop of one-half year in the average years of schooling for Puerto Ricans (due undoubtedly to the low educational attainment of recent immigrants). In 1950, the average income of Negro men and women was $100 more than that received by Puerto Ricans. In 1960, the differential, on a family basis, rose to $400 in favor of the Negro. Conceivably the figures for Puerto Ricans are depressed by immigrants who must go through the process of Americanization.

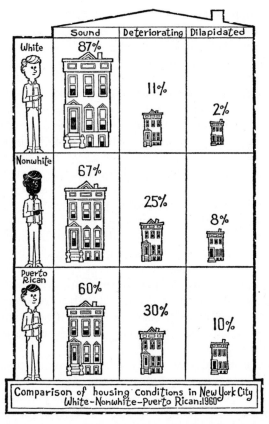

	Sound	Deteriorating	Dilapidated
White	87%	11%	2%
Nonwhite	67%	25%	8%
Puerto Rican	60%	30%	10%

Comparison of housing conditions in New York City
White–Nonwhite–Puerto Rican:1960

Table vi-9. *U.S. Censuses of Population and Housing: 1960*, Census Tract Report for New York City.

Were they better off in Puerto Rico?

A report issued several years ago by the Bureau of Applied Social Research at Columbia University argued that the average Puerto Rican "would prefer living on his island if he were able to find there the kind of economic opportunity which exists in New York." It does seem that Puerto Ricans come to New York primarily because of anticipated economic gain. They leave their island voluntarily, and in numbers that accelerate when times are good in the States and jobs are plentiful. To what extent are their expectations realized?

There are many opinions on the subject, but few objective answers. Christopher Rand in *The Puerto Ricans* reports: "One often hears that Puerto Ricans can earn twice as much in New York as on their island, and that living costs in the two places differ little except for the items of fuel and warm clothes in the New York winter." He recognizes this as a probable exaggeration but concludes that "by and large more can be made in New York (in good times)—and more can be saved, too, or spent on TV sets or washing machines." This judgment is not supported by the census results. The census was taken in Puerto Rico at the same time as in the States, using roughly the same definitions and procedures. This provides a comparison between Puerto Ricans living in New York City and those living in San Juan, the largest city on the Island.

It turns out that family income is higher in New York by 60 percent: $3,800 against $2,300 (see Table VI-10). But rents are also much higher—70 percent—and the quality of housing is much worse. On this basis it seems unlikely that *real* incomes—money incomes adjusted for differences in the cost of living—actually are higher in New York.

Housing is not only a major item in the cost of living, but also an excellent indicator of levels of living. It also happens to be one of the few items for which objective comparisons can be made between New York and San Juan. Therefore it may prove worthwhile to examine the results carefully. All but a handful of Puerto

Table VI-10   *Puerto Rican family incomes: New York City vs. San Juan in 1959*

Income level	New York	San Juan
Under $2,000	16%	43%
Between $2,000 and $4,000	38	28
Between $4,000 and $6,000	27	13
$6,000 and over	20	15
Median income	$3,800	$2,300

U.S. Census of Population: 1960, Census Tract Report for New York City; and *Detailed Characteristics, Puerto Rico*, Table 119.

Ricans living in New York reside in rented units and 40 percent of these units have one or more major defects. In San Juan, only about half of the families live in rented units and an equal number either own their homes or are in the process of buying them. These homes, incidentally, are not shacks by any means. The great majority of them are in sound condition and contain complete plumbing facilities. Even if home ownership is ignored and only the total picture is examined, it appears that Puerto Ricans in San Juan have better housing than those in New York. About the same proportion in both places live in dilapidated homes; but nearly three-fourths of the San Juan residents live in sound structures as compared with only 60 percent of the New Yorkers.

The census findings are confirmed by impressions of on-the-spot observers. Christopher Rand reports: "New stucco or cement dwellings can be seen everywhere, and public-housing projects galore can be seen in the towns—San Juan, with its suburbs, is sometimes called the world's best-endowed city now in regard to public housing."

Table VI-11   *Puerto Rican housing: New York City vs. San Juan in 1960*

Condition of housing	New York	San Juan			
		Total	Owner occupied		Renter occupied
			Land and building	Building only	
Number of units	156,000	96,000	29,000	18,000	49,000
Sound	60%	72%	91%	45%	70%
Deteriorating	30	18	7	32	19
Dilapidated	10	10	2	23	11

U.S. Censuses of Population and Housing: 1960, Census Tract Report for New York City; and *U.S. Census of Housing: 1960, Advance Reports*, Puerto Rico, HC (A2)—53, Table 1.

Those who rent get a better deal in San Juan. The overall average is $36 per month, against $62 in New York. And San Juan rents are more responsive to the quality of the housing, covering a wide range: $48 for sound housing, $26 for deteriorating units, $18 for dilapidated units. In New York, Puerto Ricans paid high rentals for all grades of housing; the comparable figures were $64, $59, and $56.

Other costs of living may also be higher in New York. Clothing requirements are undoubtedly greater, and the expense of establishing a foothold in a new environment must be counted.

These comparisons seem to downgrade the economic explanation for Puerto Rican immigration. There appears to be no great immediate advantage in moving from San Juan to New York. The figures don't tell the complete story, however.

Only *average* real income seems to be about the same in both places. Many families are below the average. These may be the ones who migrate. To the extent that this is true, New York is getting selected immigrants—people who could not make the grade in their own home towns.

Another fact to remember is that San Juan has a population of about 600,000 out of nearly 2½ million on the island. About half the people live in rural areas where incomes are very low. A substantial portion of the migrants undoubtedly come from these rural areas. They may move to New York rather than to San Juan because they have only unskilled services to offer and New York may provide a better market for those services.

Thus, while real income levels may be the same, *on the average*, in both places, the income levels among prospective migrants may be substantially worse on the island. To test this theory, much more information—and more comparable information—about conditions in Puerto Rico and New York would be needed.

Spanish-Americans

Those of us who live on the Eastern Seaboard—and this still includes about one out of every three Americans —know very little about the three and a half million people who are identified by the Census Bureau as "persons with Spanish surname." These people live in the southwestern part of the United States and in 1960 were distributed as follows: Arizona 194,000; California 1,400,000; Colorado 157,000; New Mexico 269,000; and Texas 1,400,000.

Early in the sixteenth century, the Spaniards conquered the territory that is now the American Southwest. The largest and earliest settlements were in New Mexico, but there were also others in California and Texas. This group, sometimes identified as Spanish-American or Hispano, lived in the territory that came under the American flag by the annexation of Texas, the Treaty of Guadalupe Hidalgo, and the Gadsden Purchase. Beginning about 1910, a second major group, consisting of immigrants from Mexico and their children, was added. Direct immigration from other Spanish-speaking countries has been negligible.

Ethnically, the population of Spanish-American and Mexican descent ranges from Indians to those of unmixed Spanish ancestry. Indians and the part-Spanish, part-Indian Mestizos are particularly frequent among the recent immigrant generation, the Mexican-Americans.

Special recognition of the interest in the Spanish-American and Mexican-American population of the United States was first given in the collection and publication of data on "Mexicans" in the 1930 census. These figures were collected largely because of the heavy immigration from Mexico during the twenties. Somewhat related data were collected in the 1940 census. In 1950 and 1960 white persons of Spanish-American and Mexican-American origin were identified on the basis of their Spanish surname. This procedure was limited to the five southwestern states referred to earlier.

Not as well-off as whites

Unlike the Puerto Ricans, who have a common origin and are concentrated in New York City, the Spanish-Americans are widely scattered and have diverse backgrounds. Over four-fifths of them are native Americans and more than half have mothers and fathers who are both native American. Thus, to a very large extent, this is an indigenous population rather than recent immigrants.

Unlike other parts of the country, nonwhites in the five southwestern states are not always predominantly Negro. In New Mexico, for example, three-fourths of the nonwhites are Indians, and in Arizona nearly two-thirds are Indians. In Texas, nonwhites are almost entirely Negro; but even in California and Colorado only three-fourths of the nonwhites are Negro. Table VI-12 has

| Table VI-12 | Regional comparison of median incomes in 1959: white—nonwhite— —Spanish-American | | | | |

Color	Ari-zona	Cali-fornia	Colo-rado	New Mexico	Texas
White	$2,996	$3,583	$2,876	$2,961	$2,632
Negro	1,622	2,528	2,289	1,751	1,167
Other non-white	1,034	3,014	2,361	1,378	1,943
Spanish-American	1,944	2,835	1,929	1,912	1,536

U.S. *Census of Population: 1960, Detailed Characteristics,* report for each state, Table 133 and Vol. II, *Persons of Spanish Surname.*

been arranged so that the incomes of Spanish-Americans can be compared separately with whites, Negroes, and other racial groups in each state. The "other" groups are predominantly Chinese and Japanese in California, American Indians in New Mexico and Arizona, and about equal numbers of American Indians and Orientals in Colorado and Texas.

The incomes of Spanish-Americans are far below those of whites in all states. In 1959, they fared poorest in Texas, where their median ($1,500) was only 58 percent of the white median, and best in California, where they had 79 percent of the white median. In the other three states their median was about 65 percent of that received by whites. The relationships in 1959 were not much different from those which prevailed ten years earlier. Although the situation was not static, no major changes appear to have taken place. During the fifties there was a slight increase in the income of Spanish-Americans relative to whites in California and Colorado and a slight decrease in Arizona.

Four-fifths of the Spanish-Americans live in California and Texas. Their relative economic position appears to be far better in California than in Texas. What factors account for the difference? Part of it is accounted for by the fact that a larger proportion in California live in urban areas where job opportunities are better and wages are higher. The "typical" Easterner thinks of Spanish-Americans as migrant farm workers. This may have been the case at one time, but it was far from true in 1960. Spanish-Americans in California and Texas are predominantly urbanites—85 percent in California and 79 percent in Texas live in urban areas.

Another factor that helps account for the higher incomes in California is the greater opportunity for employment in industry. This is particularly true for women. In California, 61 percent of the employed Spanish-American women worked in offices or in factories. In Texas, only 38 percent worked in these kinds of jobs. A much larger proportion of the women in Texas worked in the low-paying service trades. Many of them were domestics. The occupational distribution of the male labor force was much the same in both states; but it is likely that there was less discrimination in pay in California because a large proportion of the work in that state is done under government contract.

The lower incomes of Spanish-Americans in Texas may also be due to their low educational attainment in that state. Table VI-13 shows that Spanish-Americans were four and a half years behind whites in years of school completed in Texas, but only three years behind

Table VI-13   *Regional comparison of median years of education in 1960: white—nonwhite —Spanish-American*

Color	Ari-zona	Cali-fornia	Colo-rado	New Mexico	Texas
White	11.3	12.0	11.9	11.1	10.7
Nonwhite	7.7	10.8	11.2	7.9	8.7
Spanish-American	8.0	9.0	8.6	8.4	6.2

U.S. Census of Population: 1960, Detailed Characteristics, report for each state, Table 103 and Vol. II, *Persons of Spanish Surname.*

in California. Their lack of education in Texas, combined with language difficulties, may have made them ineligible for some of the better paying jobs.

Better off than nonwhites

Spanish-Americans are poorer than whites. That is a well-known fact. They are also better off than most nonwhites. That is also a fact, but it is not so well known. Spanish-Americans have generally had a very good press in the eastern part of the country. Their plight has been well publicized and considerable sympathy—well deserved—has been engendered. In the process, unfortunately, the impression has been created that their plight is worse than that of Negroes and other minority groups on the West Coast. Lyle Saunders states: "Not all Spanish-speaking are poor, but in general more of them are poor than is true for any other group. . . . While not all Spanish-speaking people live in slums . . . more of them do proportionately than any other population group." These statements were not true in 1949 when they were written, nor are they true today.

What are the facts as revealed in the census? They can be summarized as follows. Although Spanish-Americans are not as well off as whites, they are better off than Negroes (except in Colorado, where both are few in number) and Indians, and nearly as well off as Japanese and Chinese. These relationships not only existed in 1960 but they were also much the same ten years earlier.

In California, the median income of Spanish-Americans ($2,800) was about $300 above the Negro median even though Spanish-Americans were about two years behind in their schooling. In Texas, the other state with a large concentration of Negroes, the Spanish-Americans were $400 ahead of the Negro in median income—a differential of 32 percent. Here again the economic advantage of the Spanish-American was maintained despite a two-and-a-half-year disadvantage in schooling.

The difference between the incomes of Spanish-Americans and Indians is even greater than that cited above. Despite a doubling in the average income of Indians in Arizona during the fifties, the Spanish-American was still $900 ahead in 1959. In New Mexico the average income of Indians also doubled during the fifties, but the Spanish-American was still $500 ahead in 1959.

Orientals were the only large minority group on the West Coast that had higher incomes than Spanish-Americans. But the difference was not very great. The median for Japanese and Chinese in California was $3,000; for Spanish-Americans it was $2,800.

Quality of housing

The low economic status of Spanish-Americans and nonwhites in the western states is reflected in the poor quality of their housing. Conditions were best in California, which is considered one of the most progressive states with respect to social services. Yet even in this state two out of every ten Spanish-American and nonwhite families were living in homes that were either badly run down or dilapidated. Only one out of ten whites in the state resided in homes this bad. Conditions were much worse in Texas. There four out of every ten families in these minority groups lived in substandard homes.

Living conditions for Spanish-Americans and nonwhites were somewhat better in Colorado and New Mexico than in Texas; but the housing in Arizona was far worse than in any of the other states shown. Five out of every ten Indian families in this state lived in deteriorating or dilapidated homes. This was over three times the rate shown for white families. The low incomes and poor housing of the Indians in Arizona suggest that the opening sentence of the Meriam Report is as valid in 1960 as it was thirty-five years ago, when it was written: "An overwhelming majority of the Indians are poor, even extremely poor, and they are not adjusted to the economic and social system of the dominant white civilization."

Table VI-14   *Regional comparison of housing in 1960: white—nonwhite —Spanish-American*

Condition of housing	Arizona	California	Colorado	New Mexico	Texas
White					
Sound	86%	91%	87%	87%	83%
Deteriorating	10	7	10	9	12
Dilapidated	4	2	2	4	4
Nonwhite					
Sound	49%	80%	69%	68%	61%
Deteriorating	26	15	27	18	27
Dilapidated	25	5	4	14	12
Spanish-American					
Sound	62%	78%	66%	71%	61%
Deteriorating	24	16	26	18	26
Dilapidated	14	6	8	11	13

U.S. Census of Population: 1960, Summary of census tract reports for Standard Metropolitan Statistical Areas for each state.

Jew, Catholic, Protestant

About 66 percent of the population in the United States is Protestant, 26 percent is Catholic, and 3 percent is Jewish. The remaining 5 percent include people of other religions, those who profess no religious affiliation, and those who did not report their religion. In this section we shall focus on the three largest religious groups and see what differences there are in economic status as reflected in education, occupation, and income.

The Jews are one minority group in America who are not economically underprivileged. The influx of Jewish migration started toward the end of the last century. The great majority of them came with literally nothing but the shirts on their backs. Professor Will Herberg states in *Protestant-Catholic-Jew* that most of them "went into shops and factories, in light industry, or in building and allied trades; they became wage workers and built up a very considerable labor movement. But this process of proletarianization was not a lasting one; almost immediately a reverse process of deproletarianization set in. . . . Some of them very soon left the shop to go into business; others proved able to combine long hours in the sweatshop with after-work study that gained them coveted degrees and licenses in medicine, law, and accountancy." The way in which these people have flourished in America is a tribute to themselves and to the United States.

Income

The average income of Jewish household heads was considerably higher than that of Protestants or Catholics.

About one out of every five Jewish family heads has an income over $10,000 as compared with one out of twenty for Catholics and Protestants. Overall, Catholics have higher income than Protestants, largely because they are more concentrated in larger cities and work at non-farm jobs.

Table VI-15   *Income and religion of household heads: Protestant—Catholic—Jew, 1953–1955*

Income level	Protestant	Catholic	Jewish
Under $2,000	19%	12%	9%
Between $2,000 and $4,000	32	30	18
Between $4,000 and $5,000	17	20	12
Between $5,000 and $7,500	20	25	32
Between $7,500 and $10,000	6	8	11
$10,000 and over	5	5	19

Donald J. Bogue, *The Population of the United States,* Free Press of Glencoe, Illinois, 1959.

The higher incomes of Jewish family heads are in large measure due to the fact that they are better educated. Most of the well-paid jobs in our society require college training or high-level managerial or technical responsibility. Since a large proportion of the Jewish family heads are college-trained and work at professional and managerial jobs, it is not surprising that many of them are in the upper income brackets.

	Protestant	Catholic	Jewish
Elementary School	37%	41%	26%
High School	43%	43%	41%
1 to 3 years College	11%	9%	11%
4 years or more College	9%	7%	22%

Education and Religion: Protestant—Catholic—Jew 1953–1955

Table VI-16. Source: same as Table VI-15.

Education

The figures on educational attainment show that the proportion of college men is far greater among the Jews than it is in either of the two other groups shown. One out of every five Jewish family heads is a college graduate. This proportion is twice that among Protestants and three times the Catholic rate. Protestants have somewhat higher college attendance rates than Catholics, but the difference in education between the two groups is not very striking.

Occupations

The figures on occupational distribution show that the Jews have not only acquired education, but that they have also been given the opportunity to use their training. More than two out of every five Jewish family heads are professional or managerial workers. These are the two highest paying major occupation groups. The comparable proportion for Catholics and Protestants was one out of five. The second most important occupation group for Jews was clerical and sales. About one-fourth of the family heads worked in these occupations. Altogether about 70 percent of the Jewish family heads worked in white-collar jobs as compared with only one-third for Protestants and Catholics.

The major difference in occupational distribution between the two Christian religions is the greater concentration of Protestants in agricultural jobs. About 13 percent of the Protestants were farmers as compared with only 5 percent of the Catholics. There is a correspondingly greater proportion of Catholics in blue-collar jobs, reflecting their greater concentration in urban areas.

Table VI-17	Occupation and religion of household heads: Protestant—Catholic—Jew, 1953–1955		
Major occupation group	Protestant	Catholic	Jewish
Professional or managerial worker	21%	21%	44%
Farmer	13	5	1
Clerical or sales worker	11	11	26
Craftsman	19	22	7
Semiskilled	20	24	12
Service worker or laborer	16	16	1

Source: same as Table VI-15.

CHAPTER VII

Who, me? In the top income groups?

We hear a lot about the poor. Congressional com-
mittees study their characteristics and devise programs
for their help. They are the focal point of discussions
about crime, juvenile delinquency, slums, school dropouts,
and many other social problems. This is as it should be.
We are a people with a conscience and we deplore the
existence of poverty. President Kennedy stated the issue
squarely when he told Congress: "There is a claim on our
conscience from . . . the elderly, nonwhites, migratory
workers, and the physically or mentally handicapped—
people who are shortchanged even in time of prosperity."

But how about the rich? What are they like? Their
characteristics and behavior are in many ways just as
important to society as are those of the poor—not because
of what we can do for them, but because of what they
can do for us. They own most of the wealth, do most of
the saving, and are primarily responsible for investments,
which are the key to prosperity and full employment.
There are, to be sure, some wealthy people that society
could get along very well without, but, by and large, the
wealthy in the United States contain some of the best and
most essential talents—doctors, lawyers, engineers, enter-
tainers, artists, plant managers, etc. While the association
between ability and income is far from perfect, ordinary
observation shows that many of the most talented are included among the highest paid.

Aside from the economic importance of the rich,

there is ample evidence that most people have an idle curiosity about what they do and what they are like.

Who is rich?

The most famous economics textbook of them all, Samuelson's *Economics*, begins the discussion of family income like this:

> F. Scott Fitzgerald: You know, Ernest, the rich are different from us.
> Ernest Hemingway: Yes, I know. They have more money than we do.

Are the rich really so much like other people that the only difference is their money? It is hard to say without a more precise definition of terms. Who is rich? Men who earn as much as $30,000 or $40,000 a year often do not regard themselves as rich because their friends and neighbors earn so much more. Many people with incomes this high complain that after taxes and "necessary" expenses, they have very little left over. Very often, salaried professional men, small businessmen, and even government workers, who regard themselves as comfortable, but not well-to-do, are simply amazed when they look at an income distribution and find that they are in the top 1 or 2 percent income brackets. They just don't feel that well off and would vociferously deny that they are at the top of the heap.

Since the rich cannot be objectively defined, arbitrary standards must be used. Government statistics show the characteristics of the wealthiest 5 percent of the families at different points in time. Some figures are also available for the top 1 percent. These numbers will be used, not only to show the composition of this top group in 1960 but also to show how it changed during the preceding decade. And it did change!

This group is not the rich-rich, by any means. In 1960 families with as little as $25,000 a year would have been included in the top 1 percent, and those with more than $15,000 were in the top 5 percent. A decade earlier all that was needed was about $10,000 to qualify for the top 5 percent. A higher point on the income scale—say $50,000 or more—would have made a much better baseline for discussion of the rich. But there are no reliable figures for the rich-rich at present and so we must make do with what we have. Even these figures mirror several significant changes whose full impact has not yet been generally appreciated.

Work is the rule

If you believe that there are large numbers in this top group who make their living by clipping coupons, you couldn't be farther from the truth. In 1960, only one family out of a hundred in the top 5 percent lived entirely on unearned income—interest, dividends, rents, royalties, and the like. The other ninety-nine did paid work or were self-employed, and in the great majority of cases were largely dependent on the income they received from their jobs or businesses. In fact, one-third of the total lived entirely on earned income and received nothing from investments—at least nothing that they considered large enough to report to the census interviewer.

Even higher on the income ladder there is no appreciable difference in this picture. For 1960, figures are available for the top 1 percent of the families—those making $25,000 a year or more. Only three out of every hundred of these families lived entirely on unearned income.

The great majority of families in the top 5 percent income group are there because they are headed by a man whose skills are much in demand and who therefore has high earning potential. It would be a mistake, however, to assume that only the husbands work in these families and that the wives and children enjoy a life of luxurious ease. On the contrary, one out of every four families in this group has a working wife—the very same proportion as the national average.

Among the top 1 percent, working wives are somewhat less numerous. But, even at this level, one out of every six wives had a paid job. Why do they work? The reason varies. If you ask them, many will say, "For the money." But that is only part of the answer, and a small part. Many women who are married to successful men are well trained themselves and are not satisfied to do menial jobs around the house or to bask in the glory of their husbands' accomplishments. They seek personal and intellectual independence and often find it in a job.

Dad works, Mother works, and in many cases other relatives in the home also work in the top income groups. One-fourth of the families in the top 5 percent had three or more workers in 1960. Many of these families never would have qualified for inclusion were it not for the fact that the pooling of several average incomes together created an above-average income for the family.

The kind of work they do

The most distinctive feature about the top 5 percent is the kind of work they do. This characteristic, more than any other, sets them apart from the rest of society. It is also most revealing about the changes that have taken place in this group during the fifties.

The pictograph below (Table VII-1) shows that in 1950 the dominant group within the top 5 percent were the self-employed. They accounted for over two-fifths of the total. By 1960, the importance of this group was greatly reduced, to only one-fourth. White-collar and manual workers were also reduced in importance as a component of the top income group.

In contrast, salaried managerial and professional workers, who essentially represent "brain power," rose considerably in importance between 1950 and 1960. In the earlier period they represented only 28 percent of the total, whereas in 1960 they made up nearly 50 percent.

A closer look at the changes for specific groups shows that, within the self-employed category, doctors, dentists, lawyers, and other independent professionals held their own. Farmers dropped sharply, as might be expected in this declining occupation and owners of small businesses also dropped sharply.

Some will argue that the distinction between the owner of an unincorporated business and the salaried corporation official is nebulous. Technically, the corner groceryman would appear in the figures as the owner of a business if he is unincorporated. Should he incorporate (upon the advice of his son-in-law, the accountant) he immediately becomes a salaried corporation official. It is generally believed that there is a tendency for small firms to become incorporated in order to take advantage of the tax laws, or the limited liability provided by the corporate form of organization. According to the census figures, however, there was no great general movement from proprietorship toward incorporation during the fifties. In 1950, about 8 percent of *all* family heads were classified as owners of unincorporated businesses. In 1960,

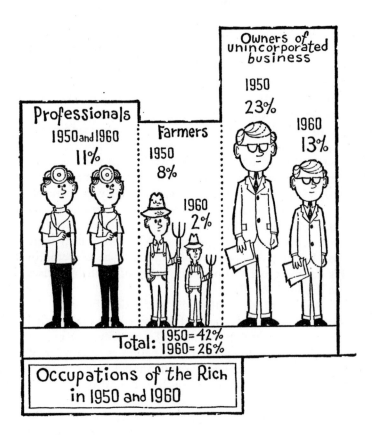

Owners of unincorporated business

1950
23%

1960
13%

Professionals
1950 and 1960
11%

Farmers
1950
8%

1960
2%

Total: 1950=42%
1960=26%

Occupations of the Rich
in 1950 and 1960

the comparable figure was 7 percent—no change to speak of. But, within the top income group, owners of unincorporated businesses dropped from 23 percent of the total to only 13 percent. In other words, there were proportionately about as many small businessmen in 1960 as

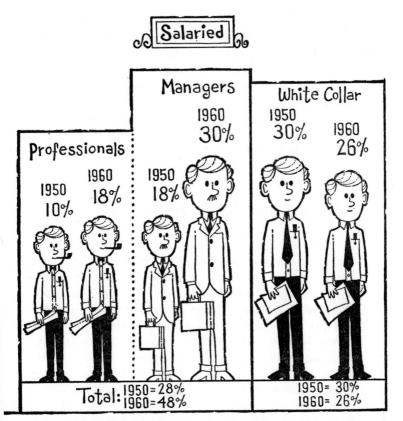

Table VII-1. U.S. Bureau of the Census, *Trends in the Income of Families and Persons in the United States, 1947 to 1960*. Technical Paper No. 8, 1963, p. 23.

there were in 1950, but they were more concentrated in the lower income levels.

The same picture appears when the figures for salaried managers and officials are examined. In 1950 about 6 percent of all family heads were in this occupation, as compared with about 8 percent in 1960. However, their representation in the top income group increased from 18 percent to 30 percent.

The other striking and significant fact shown in the pictograph (Table VII-1) is the increase in the relative importance of salaried professional workers in the top income group. In 1960, there were more salaried professionals at all income levels than there were in 1950; but the increase was greatest at the top.

Significance of the big change

The big change is the persistent intrusion of brain power into the top 5 percent. The small businessman and the farmer have given way to the engineer, scientist, college professor, plant manager, and others who deal primarily with ideas, not things. It was not too many years ago that Professor Morris R. Cohen, eminent philosopher of the College of the City of New York, proclaimed: "Mankind has been ruled by soldiers, clergy, and lawyers, and now the businessmen control." Babbitt has not yet been dethroned, but he sits uneasily on his throne.

There was a time, not too long ago, when all you needed to operate a small business was a little money, a little experience, and lots of luck. Many failed, but the successful gained entry into the top income group. Some people still get to the top that way, but their number is dwindling. Small business has been taken over by the big corporation; but the change does not end there. The corporation executive today is often more than just an administrator. He must also be qualified to handle complex technical problems. Many of the people who are now called managers or officials are in reality scientists or engineers. Indeed, it is not at all unusual to find engineers and scientists directing the activities of huge corporations; and, what is more important, many who have purely technical responsibilities earn as much as or more than their bosses.

The editors of *Fortune* magazine wrote not too long ago: "The tycoon is dead. . . . The mid-century businessman has had to go to school—in labor, in politics, in social welfare. The engineer's a businessman, the salesman's an economist, the research man knows advertising, the finance man knows law." In much the same vein, historian Frederick Lewis Allen in *The Big Change* stated: "There is a striking difference between the type of men now rising to the top in big business and those of an earlier day. . . . Nowadays it seems quite natural to us that the great majority of big business executives should be college graduates and that many should have been trained in engineering or law."

What is true for big business is equally true for big government. Twenty-five years ago Washington, D.C., was almost a sleepy southern town. There were some mathematicians, physicists, and statisticians but they were few in number and hard to find. The typical government executive was a political appointee or a clerk who worked his way up through the ranks. My, how things have changed! The government executive today is invariably college trained and very often an acknowledged expert in his field. He is almost always supported by a team of experts who earn nearly as much as he does.

When the Census Bureau purchased its first electronic computer around 1950, it found that it also had to hire a young engineer to keep the blasted thing going. He was paid a base salary that nearly equaled that of the Director of the Census. With overtime payments, he earned more than the Secretary of Commerce. And so it goes in many organizations.

Automation, computers, research—these all require

skill and brains which are great in demand and short in supply. That is the simple explanation behind the rapid growth in brain power within the top income group.

A glimpse at the assets of the top groups

Little is known about the characteristics of the rich-rich. This is not because of any diabolical plot to keep their financial information a secret. The reason for our ignorance is much simpler. The number of people who receive very high incomes is quite small: there were only 28,000 individual income tax returns with incomes over $100,000 in 1959. This number is so small that the characteristics of the group cannot be identified in the nation-wide sample surveys that provide the information for the top 5 percent and the top 1 percent. Specially designed sample surveys are needed for this group, but such surveys have never been made in the United States. The figures in the pictograph (Table VII-2) are based on a small-scale study conducted in 1960 by the Bureau of the Census for the Federal Reserve Board. About six hundred families with incomes between $7,500 and $15,000, and another six hundred with incomes of $15,000 or more, were interviewed concerning their income, assets, debts, and investments. This survey was not intended to be representative of the nation as a whole. On the contrary, it was concentrated in a few residential areas of four large cities, where it was expected that families would be found with investment portfolios larger and more complex than the average. This choice was made because such a group provided an efficient means of studying savings practices. The survey provides a very rough idea of the financial characteristics of the top income groups.

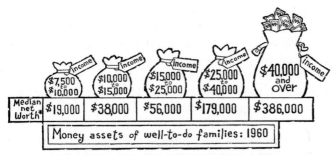

Money assets of well-to-do families: 1960

* Net worth is the sum of the value of assets less debts. The following assets were included in the survey: liquid assets (checking and savings accounts, shares in mutual funds, credit balances in brokerage accounts); stocks; marketable bonds; mortgage and other loan assets; equity in an unincorporated business; investment real estate; own home; cash surrender value of life insurance; beneficial interests in estates and trusts; and individual annuities.

Table VII-2. Board of Governors of the Federal Reserve System, *Special Survey of Financial Characteristics: Special Report to Respondents*, September 29, 1961.

You don't have to move very far up the income scale to find families whose average net worth is quite high. Families with incomes from $7,500–$10,000 can hardly be regarded as well-to-do; yet the pictograph (Table VII-2) shows that their median net worth was about $19,000.

The $15,000–$25,000 income class is quite high by most standards, but it does not represent the rich-rich. Yet the median net worth for this class was $56,000. The top 1 percent of the families, those with incomes over $25,000, had a median net worth of about one-quarter of a million dollars.

If your net worth is average or above average for your income class, you have some idea of how families at that income class have managed to accumulate their assets. However, many families, including a large proportion of those with incomes between $10,000 and $25,000, do not have large asset holdings. To these families, the whole process of building up a large net worth on a limited income is one of life's puzzles. But the figures are not very hard to understand or to believe once you get down to particular cases. Take, for example, the hypothetical case of Frank and Edna K. of Cleveland, Ohio.

If you visited this couple in their home or met them in the street or the supermarket, you would never guess that they are worth $135,000. They are both in their sixties and have been in the retail hardware business all their married life. Mr. K. grew up on a farm in the Midwest. He quit school in the fourth grade and worked on his father's farm until he was seventeen. He served in World War I and when he was discharged he went to Cleveland instead of returning to the farm. There he met and married Mrs. K. Shortly after their marriage, they opened up a small hardware store.

In 1962, Mr. and Mrs. K. had a joint income of $15,000 from their business. This was their only source of income. Mr. K. estimated the value of his business at $85,000. He also owned $50,000 worth of residential property that was not yet providing him a rental income. The only other assets the K.'s had was a joint checking account of $2,000 and life insurance policies with cash values of about $3,000. The K.'s had sold their home when their children got married, so they had no equity in a home. They also had no stocks or bonds; Mr. K. had a morbid fear of paper assets as a result of having gone broke during the depression. The only debt the K.'s had was a $5,000 bank note representing a loan they had made to help their son go into business. Thus, although the K.'s had an income of only $15,000 a year, their assets were worth $135,000.

The S. family of Baltimore, Maryland, provides another hypothetical illustration of a $15,000-a-year family with relatively large assets. John S. is in his fifties and is the manager of an insurance company. He is a college graduate as is his wife Susan. They have two boys aged seventeen and fourteen. This family had an income of $15,250 in 1962, almost entirely from wages and salaries received by John. Yet they live in a $35,000 house, which has a $15,000 mortgage. Thus the equity in their house was $20,000. In addition, John owns $20,000 worth of residential real estate, $10,000 worth of common stocks, and life insurance policies with cash surrender values of $10,000. The family also has savings and checking accounts that total about $3,000. They have no debts, so the total value of their assets is $63,000. Most of these assets were accumulated shortly after World War II. John had been in the insurance business before he entered the service and he knew about investments. He felt that there would be a big inflation of prices after the war and he invested all of his money in common stocks. He proved to be right and now has started diversifying his assets into residential property and other forms of investment.

If you met Mr. Sol W., a government clerk, on the street, he would impress you as anything but a man of means. Although his annual income was only $8,000 in 1962, his assets were worth about $50,000. Mr. W. is a widower. He and his wife worked for the government all their lives. Mrs. W. died in 1958. Mr. W.'s home was completely paid for and was valued at $25,000. He has about $14,000 in government bonds, which he bought largely with the money from Mrs. W.'s pension-fund contributions, which were willed to him upon his wife's death. Mr. W. also has a savings account of about $7,000 and policies that have cash surrender value of $3,000. He has no debts to speak of; so his net worth is $49,000.

A little deeper probe into the characteristics of the top income groups is provided in Table VII-3. At the lowest income level for which data are shown ($7,500 to $10,000) one-half of the assets represented equity in homes or the surrender value of life insurance policies. Stocks accounted for only 17 percent of the total and interest in business only 11 percent. As income rises, the relative importance of home ownership and life insurance declines, and stocks and business ownership assume much greater significance. Thus, at the top income level ($40,000 and over), business ownership accounted for 43 percent of the total value of assets, and stock ownership accounted for 28 percent of the total. Together, these two items accounted for $7 out of every $10 in assets held by the top income group.

Table VII-3   *Sources of assets of well-to-do families in 1960*

Family income	Stock	Other financial assets	Equity in business	Equity in own home	Life insurance (surrender value)	Other
Between $7,500 and $10,000	17%	15%	11%	44%	8%	5%
Between $10,000 and $15,000	19	16	21	29	6	9
Between $15,000 and $25,000	18	15	31	21	6	9
Between $25,000 and $40,000	27	14	32	13	4	11
$40,000 and over	28	13	43	7	2	7

Board of Governors of the Federal Reserve System, *Special Survey of Financial Characteristics: Special Report to Respondents*, September 29, 1961.

CHAPTER VIII

The cash value of education

"Let ignorance talk as it will, learning has its value." Thus wrote the French essayist La Fontaine three hundred years ago. He was so right. Every study of the relation between earnings and education shows that the more highly educated the man, the greater his earnings. There are many exceptions to be sure. Differences in talent, home environment, family connections, drive, imagination, and just plain old luck cause some people to do well and others poorly. And immaterial factors—the color of a man's skin, for example—make education more worthwhile to some than to others.

Perhaps it is regrettable to stress the value of education in such crass terms. Education tends to produce a richer and more varied life and it is fundamental to the operation of a democratic society. For these reasons alone, it is worth its cost in time, money, and effort even if the economic advantages should cease to exist. The main reason for focusing on the economic advantages is a simple one. At present, they are the only ones that can be measured even approximately.

But there is at least one more reason for stressing the pay-off from education—to convince our poor, whose children are badly in need of schooling, that it may be a way out of their present dilemma. There are still many in our society who have had little experience with education and they do not see how it can help them. It is a simple point, but a fundamental one that is often overlooked. Many social workers have observed that the poor today lack the interest in education that characterized the immigrant poor who lived in the same slums twenty or thirty years ago. If this is the case, it could perpetuate the vicious circle which transmits poverty from one generation to the next. This point is well made in Christopher Rand's study *The Puerto Ricans:* "The Jewish immigrants felt that success would come through education . . . and the Italians were somewhat the same. In the garment trade twenty years ago a high percentage of the workers had kids going through college, but this is no longer the case. . . . You don't have a ferment these days to get out of the slums by educational achievement, but by financial achievement, and the Puerto Ricans reflect this. The Puerto Rican kids here dream of quick money, not of intellectual attainments." Rand's observation undoubtedly applies to Negroes as well.

There is some justification for the feeling by Puerto Ricans, Negroes, and other minority groups that education does not do as much for them, financially, as it does for others. James Baldwin writes in *Nobody Knows My Name:* "It is not to be wondered at that a boy, one day, decides that if . . . studying is going to prepare him only to be a porter or an elevator boy—or his teacher—well, then, the hell with it."

The figures below show that nonwhites (largely Negroes) who have completed four years of college, *can expect to earn only as much in a lifetime as whites who have not gone beyond the eighth grade.* And this applies not only to the South, but to the North as well. No wonder nonwhites show little enthusiasm for schooling. Indeed, it is surprising that so many have continued with their education until the average nonwhite man in his twenties is now only about one and a half years behind the white in years of schooling.

Emphasis on the negative aspects of the situation, important though it may be as a stimulus to improvement, should not obscure an equally important fact—that schooling does pay off for nonwhites, even though the amount is far less than for whites. And even if it did not pay off today, it is still important if nonwhites are ever to advance out of their low economic status.

An investment in education is much like buying insurance. No insurance company can tell you how long you are going to live; but they do know your chances of living a given number of years if they know your age, sex, and several other things about you. The same thing holds for education. No one can tell you how much you will earn in a lifetime on the basis of your education. We can estimate your chances.

The figures in the pictograph (Table VIII-I) show the average amount of money earned per year by men with different amounts of schooling. Several different periods during the past twenty years are listed to show how the relationship has changed.

Women have been excluded from the figures because a large proportion of them do not enter the labor market and many of those who do are employed on a part-time basis only. Although education has a direct impact on the income of those women who work, its value is much more indirect for the large proportion who do not work. To most girls education provides a greater opportunity to marry a man who will be financially successful; it also provides more in the way of intangibles that may be more important than money—the kind of man she may marry, her influence on his life, the environment for her children, etc. In contrast, practically all adult men are full-time workers; advantages which accrue from more schooling are reflected in their incomes.

In every year for which data are shown the completion of an additional level of schooling was associated with higher average incomes. In 1959, elementary school graduates made $3,800, high school graduates made $5,600, and college graduates made $9,200. In that one year the difference between the incomes of the average high school and the average college graduate was considerably greater than the cost of a year of college. This finding parallels that obtained in numerous other studies dating back to the early part of this century.

Although the income levels have changed considerably during the past twenty years, the basic relationship between the extent of schooling and income appears to have remained much the same. These facts belie the dire expectations of some analysts—"a college degree isn't worth anything any more." They also show how wrong were those men who opposed the vast expansion of college training programs after World War II. Professor Seymour Harris of Harvard wrote in 1949 that the persistent increase in the supply of college-trained workers would so flood the market that "college students within the next twenty years are doomed to disappointment after graduation, as the number of coveted openings will be substantially less than the numbers seeking them." The same concern was expressed by James B. Conant, then president of Harvard, and Chancellor William J. Wallin of the New York State Board of Regents.

These gloomy warnings were fortunately ignored. At some risk and considerable expense, the schooling of the American population increased tremendously during the postwar years. The demand for these more highly trained workers has kept pace with the supply so that they are, by and large, fully employed.

Although income generally tends to increase with education, the completion of a given level of schooling (e.g., the fourth year in high school) yields a greater return than any of the years leading up to graduation. This difference may reflect a selection in terms of ability be-

Elementary School	1939	1949	1959
Less than 8 years	figures not available	$2,062	$2,551
8 years	figures not available	$2,829	$3,769
High School 1 to 3 years	$1,379	$3,226	$4,618
4 years	$1,661	$3,784	$5,567
College 1 to 3 years	$1,931	$4,423	$6,966
4 years or more	$2,607	$6,179	$9,206

Education and income
Men: 1939, 1949, and 1959

Table VIII-1. Herman P. Miller, "Annual and Lifetime Income in Relation to Education: 1939–1959," *American Economic Review*, December, 1960, Table 1. The pictograph shows average incomes for men aged 25 and over.

tween those who do and those who do not complete
their schooling. Or it may represent the commercial
value of a certificate or title. Thus in 1959, men who
started high school but did not graduate received on the
average an annual income of about $800 more per year
than men who left school after the eighth grade. High
school graduates, however, received about $900 more of
annual income per year than high school dropouts.

Schooling pays—even for a bricklayer

Everyone knows that it pays to go to college. But
does schooling pay off if you are only going to be a carpenter, a plumber, or a bus driver? Definitely. The figures
in the pictograph (Table viii-2) below show the earnings
of two groups of white males in their prime years. Nonwhites and men in other age groups are omitted in order
to focus on one thing only—the effect of education on
earnings. One group never went beyond the eighth grade
and the other group finished high school. The figures
show that in many occupations the high school diploma
is worth about $1,000 a year—roughly $40,000 over a
working lifetime.

Why the difference? There are many reasons. High
school graduates have higher IQ's. This is partly due to
their greater education. It may also reflect greater native
intelligence and aptitude to learn. But there are other
reasons.

Employers give preference to high school graduates.
With a diploma you can drive a bus for a transcontinental
bus company; without it, you're lucky to get a job with
the Podunk Transit Company. The carpenter who is a
high school graduate has a regular job with a big con-

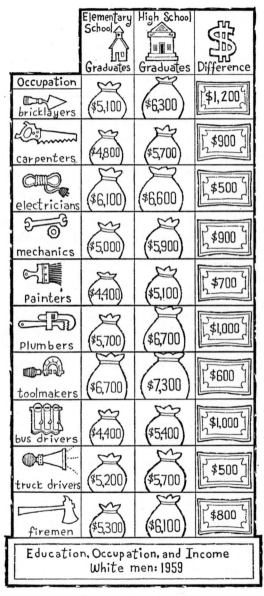

Occupation	Elementary School Graduates	High School Graduates	$ Difference
bricklayers	$5,100	$6,300	$1,200
carpenters	$4,800	$5,700	$900
electricians	$6,100	$6,600	$500
mechanics	$5,000	$5,900	$900
Painters	$4,400	$5,100	$700
Plumbers	$5,700	$6,700	$1,000
toolmakers	$6,700	$7,300	$600
bus drivers	$4,400	$5,400	$1,000
truck drivers	$5,200	$5,700	$500
firemen	$5,300	$6,100	$800

Education, Occupation, and Income
White men: 1959

Table VIII-2. *U.S. Census of Population: 1960*, Vol. II, Part 7B, *Occupation by Earnings and Education*. The pictograph shows average earnings of white men aged 35 to 44.

struction firm. He works regularly, good weather and bad. The uneducated carpenter works by the day. He gets a job, finishes it, and goes down to the union hall to get another. Whenever work is slack, he is the first to go.

Unions also prefer high school graduates. Increasingly, the diploma is becoming a prerequisite to qualify for apprentice training. According to one study "virtually all registered apprenticeship programs require a minimum of two years of high school education or its equivalent. Skills are becoming more complex, and so is related classroom training, an essential ingredient in all registered apprenticeship programs. Many apprenticeship programs, therefore, are raising their educational standards and accepting nothing less than a high school diploma or its equivalent." An official of the General Electric Company reports that at one time the Schenectady plant "used to screen applicants by means of a simple test based on the three R's. Now the company accepts only apprentices who have high school diplomas and who have earned superior grades in mathematics and science."

The reasons are varied, but the facts are clear. Education pays off.

Lifetime earnings

Estimates of lifetime earnings provide better measures of financial returns associated with education than the annual earnings shown above. Table VIII-1 shows that the difference in average income between high school and college graduates in one year was more than enough to pay for the cost of a year in college. So you can well imagine that the difference in income over a lifetime will be enormous.

The figures on lifetime earnings in Table VIII-3 are

146

prepared according to standard techniques of life insurance practice. The procedure can best be explained by the following numerical example.

STEP 1 Out of every 100,000 male children born in 1959, 95,716 could expect to survive to age 18.

STEP 2 Out of 95,716 who survive to 18, 94,591 will survive to age 24. Between the ages of 18 and 24 they will have lived 666,226 man-years. Assume that each year they receive average (mean) earnings of $2,731. (This is the arithmetic mean earnings reported in the 1960 census for men 18 to 24 years old.) Total expected earnings from age 18 to 24 is $1.8 billion.

STEP 3 Out of 94,591 who survive to age 24, about 93,029 can be expected to survive to age 34. Between the ages of 25 and 34 they will have lived 937,542 man-years. Assuming average earnings of $5,188 per year (the amount reported in the census for men 25 to 34 years old) their total expected earnings during this period is $4.9 billion.

STEP 4 Out of the 93,029 who survive to age 34, 89,888 can be expected to survive to age 44. Their total man-years of life during this period will be 913,545. Assuming average earnings of $6,259 for each year gives them a total expected earnings of $5.7 billion.

STEP 5 Out of 89,888 who survive to age 44, 82,082 can be expected to survive to age 54. Their total man-years of life during this period will be 857,620. Assuming average earnings of $6,194 for each year gives them a total expected earnings of $5.3 billion.

STEP 6 Out of 82,082 who survive to 54 years, 66,195 can be expected to survive to age 64. Their total man-years during this period will be 732,320. Assuming average earnings of $5,737 for each year gives them a total expected earnings of $4.2 billion.

STEP 7 Adding up all of the amounts listed above leads to the conclusion that the 95,716 men who reached age 18 would have earned about $21.9 billion during their lifetime. The average for each one was therefore $229,000.

Table VIII-3   *Education and lifetime earnings: men*

(Earnings from age 18 to 64)

Highest grade completed	Earnings
All education groups	$229,000
Elementary school	
Less than 8 years	143,000
8 years	184,000
High school	
1 to 3 years	212,000
4 years	247,000
College	
1 to 3 years	293,000
4 years or more	417,000
4 years	385,000
5 years or more	455,000

Based on 1960 census figures. U.S. Senate, 88th Congress, 1st Session, *Hearings Before the Committee on Labor and Public Welfare on Bills Relating to Equal Employment Opportunities*, July and August, 1963, p. 335.

On the basis of conditions in 1959, an elementary school graduate could expect to earn during his lifetime about $41,000 more, on the average, than the person who quit before completing the eighth grade. This large difference cannot be entirely due to the completion of several additional years of elementary school. You just don't learn that much in grade school. The chances are that failure to complete elementary school is, by and large, symptomatic of other traits that lead to low productivity and low income. Here again caution must be exercised lest the figures be misunderstood, for there are exceptions.

The difference between the expected lifetime earnings of the average elementary school and high school graduate is equally striking. In 1959, the average elementary school graduate could expect lifetime earnings of about $184,000 as compared with about $247,000 for the average high school graduate—a difference of $63,000.

A college degree is required for many, if not most, high-paying jobs. And the greatest gains associated with additional schooling appear at the college level. In 1959, a college graduate could expect to earn about $417,000 during his lifetime as compared with $247,000 for the average high school graduate. During his lifetime, the average college graduate earns about $38,000 *extra* for each year of college. Even if these earnings are matched against the high cost of college training—a cost generally borne by the parents rather than the children—the rate of return is obviously substantial.

Gains are much less for nonwhites

The association between earnings and education is not the same for all groups. It would be most surprising if it were, in view of the obstacles that restrict entry of Negroes and other minorities into many of the better paying jobs.

Table VIII-4 *Education and earnings in 1959: white men vs. nonwhite men*

(Earnings from age 25 to 64)

Occupation	Elementary school graduates			High school graduates		
	White	Nonwhite	Ratio of non-white to white	White	Nonwhite	Ratio of non-white to white
Craftsmen, foremen, and kindred workers						
Overall	$5,300	$3,800	.72	$6,100	$4,500	.73
Brickmasons, stonemasons and tile setters	5,100	4,000	.78	6,100	3,900	.63
Carpenters	4,400	3,200	.72	5,400	4,100	.76
Compositors and typesetters	6,000	*	*	6,400	4,600	.72
Electricians	6,100	*	*	6,400	5,600	.87
Linemen and servicemen, telegraph, telephone, and power	5,800	*	*	6,300	5,200	.82
Machinists	5,500	4,300	.79	6,000	5,100	.85
Mechanics and repairmen	4,900	3,700	.75	5,500	4,400	.79
Painters, construction and maintenance	5,200	3,100	.73	4,800	3,500	.72
Plasterers	5,100	3,600	.72	6,400	*	*
Plumbers and pipefitters	5,600	4,000	.71	6,400	4,500	.71

Occupation	Elementary school graduates			High school graduates		
	White	Nonwhite	Ratio of non-white to white	White	Nonwhite	Ratio of non-white to white
Operatives and kindred workers						
Overall	$4,800	$3,600	.75	$5,400	$4,000	.74
Bus drivers	4,300	3,500	.81	5,100	4,700	.93
Mine operatives and laborers	4,300	3,500	.80	5,400	3,800	.70
Truck and tractor drivers	4,900	3,300	.68	5,500	3,700	.68
Operatives and kindred workers (not elsewhere classified)	4,800	3,800	.80	5,400	4,100	.77
Service workers, including private household						
Overall	3,900	2,900	.75	5,000	3,300	.66
Barbers	4,500	2,800	.62	4,900	3,500	.72
Policemen and detectives	4,800	*	*	5,500	5,200	.94

* Averages not computed for occupations with fewer than 1,000 persons with earnings.

U.S. Census of Population: 1960, Vol. II, Part 7B, *Occupation by Earnings and Education.*

An examination of the figures separately for the two racial groups shows that education pays off for each, but the returns are far greater for whites. In Table VIII-4, occupations have been selected for which annual earnings estimates are available for whites and nonwhites. In most occupations, nonwhite men earned about three-fourths as much as whites with the same amount of schooling. In nearly every occupation nonwhite high school graduates earned less than whites who never went beyond the eighth grade. The reasons for these differences undoubtedly vary according to the occupation. In the highly unionized crafts, many nonwhites may have to work for lower pay on nonunion jobs because they are not permitted to join the unions. Even when they are union members, they may not be able to get the better jobs with large companies, where they are assured of regular employment. In those occupations that are not highly unionized, nonwhite workers, regardless of education, may be the first dismissed during slack periods. As a result, their annual earnings are lower than those of whites even though they are paid at the same hourly rate.

Even when nonwhite men are educated and are employed in a trade or profession, their earnings are far below those of whites with the same number of years of schooling and doing the same kinds of work. This is one cause of the low economic status of nonwhites. A more important cause is their concentration in low-paid occupations such as laborers and service workers. This fact is clearly brought out in Table VIII-5 below, which shows the occupational distribution of white and nonwhite men by years of schooling.

A nonwhite man who has not gone beyond the eighth grade has very little chance of being anything more than a laborer, a porter, or a factory hand. Nearly eight out of every ten nonwhite men with only eight grades of schooling worked as laborers, service workers, or operatives at the time of the last census. Among whites with the same amount of education only five out of ten worked at these low-paid jobs.

The nonwhite high school graduate stands a somewhat better chance of getting a well-paid job; but even his chances are not very good. About six out of every ten nonwhite high school graduates were laborers, service workers, or operatives as compared with only three out of ten whites with the same amount of schooling.

Nonwhite college graduates seem to be able to find professional employment in relatively large numbers. About three out of every four were professional or managerial workers—nearly the same proportion as white college graduates. But there is one big difference. Nonwhites were concentrated in the lower-paid professions. One-third of the male nonwhite college graduates in professional employment were schoolteachers as compared with only one-sixth of the whites. Moreover, earnings of nonwhites in the low-paid professions were considerably below those of whites. Relatively few nonwhites are in the higher paid professions. About 20 percent of the white male college graduates in professional employment were engineers as compared with only 8 percent of the nonwhites; 14 percent of the whites were lawyers or accountants, but only 6 percent of the nonwhites. There were proportionately as many nonwhite doctors as white, but the average earnings of the nonwhites were only half that received by the whites.

The pictograph (Table VIII-6) presents figures on the lifetime earnings of white and nonwhite men by years of school completed. The life tables for each color group were used to prepare the lifetime earnings. Since whites tend to live longer than nonwhites, on the average,

Table VIII-5 *Education and occupation: white vs. nonwhite men, aged 18 to 64, in 1960*

	White			Nonwhite		
Major occupation group	Elementary school graduate	High school graduate	College graduate	Elementary school graduate	High school graduate	College graduate
Number (thousands)	5,736	10,082	4,071	488	609	145
Professional and managerial workers	9%	21%	77%	3%	7%	72%
Farmers and farm managers	9	5	1	3	2	1
Clerical and sales workers	8	20	15	4	16	13
Craftsmen, foremen, and kindred workers	28	25	4	13	15	4
Operatives and kindred workers	29	20	1	31	27	4
Service workers	6	5	1	17	18	5
Laborers	11	5	1	29	16	2

U.S. Census of Population: 1960, Vol. II, Part 7B, *Occupation by Earnings and Education.*

their lifetime incomes will also tend to be greater, regardless of schooling; they simply enjoy more years of working life. The difference in life expectancy, however, accounts for only a small part of the difference in earnings and does not substantially change the conclusions. For example, on the basis of actual experience in 1959, nonwhite men could expect lifetime earnings of about

$122,000 or about 51 percent of the white total. If non-whites had the same life expectancy as whites, their expected lifetime earnings would be about $130,000 or 55 percent of the white total.

These figures show what a difference color makes! White high school graduates can expect $62,000 more than elementary school graduates over a lifetime; for non-whites, the difference is less than half as much ($28,000). Similarly, the difference in lifetime earnings between white high school graduates and those with four years of college is $142,000; for nonwhites the difference is $34,000.

The most disturbing fact shows up in the right-hand column of Table VIII-6. The income gap between white and nonwhite *widens* as education increases. The lifetime earnings of nonwhite elementary school graduates are 64 percent of that received by the whites. At the high school level this ratio drops to 60 percent and among college graduates it is only 50 percent. *The fact is that in 1959, the average nonwhite with four years of college could expect to earn less over a lifetime than the white who did not go beyond the eighth grade.* There are some regional differentials in these figures, but they are not as great as you might imagine. The nonwhite college graduate in the South might expect to earn about $154,000 in his lifetime. The southern white who only completed the eighth grade could expect to earn about 8 percent more ($167,000). In the northern and western states, where earnings are considerably higher than in the South, the nonwhite with four years of college could expect to earn only slightly more in a lifetime ($209,000) than the white elementary school graduate ($198,000).

These findings support the belief that much of the gap between the earnings of whites and nonwhites is due to factors other than differences in training or ability. But the figures are far from conclusive in this respect.

Elementary School	White	Nonwhite	Nonwhite as percent of white
Less than 8 years	$157,000	$95,000	61%
8 years	$191,000	$123,000	64%
High School 1 to 3 years	$221,000	$132,000	60%
4 years	$253,000	$151,000	60%
College 1 to 3 years	$301,000	$162,000	54%
4 years	$395,000	$185,000	47%
5 years or more	$466,000	$246,000	53%

Education and lifetime earnings
White men vs. Nonwhite men

Table VIII-6. Earnings for men aged 18 to 64, based on 1960 census figures. U.S. Senate, 88th Congress, 1st Session, *Hearings Before the Committee on Labor and Public Welfare on Bills Relating to Equal Employment Opportunities*, July and August, 1963.

One need not be an apologist for discrimination to point out that the meaning of a year of school completed can be quite different for whites and nonwhites. In the first place, nonwhite children receive schooling of poorer quality. As a result, nonwhites who have completed the same number of years of school as whites will not be as well educated, on the average.

This problem has received intensive study by Dr. Eli Ginzberg, director of the Conservation of Human Resources Project at Columbia University. He concludes that "schools in predominantly Negro neighborhoods are in serious disrepair, are staffed by inexperienced teachers and are unable to provide instruction geared to the widely different abilities of their students." Dr. Ginzberg cites many instances that attest to the lower quality of Negro schooling. He quotes a former speaker of the House of Representatives of Georgia as saying that "what the Negro child gets in the sixth grade, the white child gets in the third grade."

You must also remember that other factors—cultural, social, and economic conditions—affect the real education a student absorbs, even in a good school. And finally, performance on the job may have little to do with training or ability. Work habits and motivation may be just as closely related to earnings as education or training.

Statistics that take all of these factors into account have yet to be devised. But figures available from the 1960 census permit a closer examination of the problem than has heretofore been possible. Shown in Table VIII-7 are the expected lifetime earnings of white and nonwhite men with less than eight years of elementary school for three occupations—carpenters, truck drivers, and semi-skilled factory workers. Since all of these men have very little schooling, it cannot be said that the whites are better educated than the nonwhites. Indeed, the low level of education for the entire group makes it likely that the great majority of these men, white and nonwhite alike, are below average in their ability to absorb formal education.

The jobs selected cover a range of skills. There are some who would argue that it is meaningless to lump all truck drivers together. The man who drives a huge diesel trailer requires entirely different skills from the deliveryman. The same argument can be made with some justification for carpenters; it cannot be validly made for semiskilled factory workers. These jobs are routine in nature and generally require little skill or experience.

The figures are shown separately for the South and for the rest of the country to take into account regional variations in earnings. The major control variables missing from the data are job performance and extent of employment. A quantitative measure of job performance cannot, of course, be obtained from census data. Figures on weeks worked were collected in the census, but were not tabulated for the groups shown below. Even if the figures were available, it is doubtful that they would contribute much to an understanding of the situation. It is very likely that nonwhites have less regularity of employment than whites. But why is this so? How much of this unemployment is involuntary and the result of discrimination? This question cannot be answered by census data.

Despite the similarity of the occupations and schooling, sharp differences persist between the earnings of whites and nonwhites. In each of the three occupations, the earnings of nonwhites in the South averaged only about two-thirds that of the whites. In the North and West the differences were somewhat narrower; but even here nonwhite carpenters and truck drivers averaged only about three-fourths of the white total. Among semiskilled factory workers nonwhites averaged about 85 percent of the white total.

Table VIII-7 — *Lifetime earnings of workers with less than eight years of schooling*

(Earnings from age 18 to 64)

Occupation	White	Nonwhite	Nonwhite as percent of white
Carpenters			
Overall	$152,000	$ 91,000	60%
South	127,000	79,000	62
North and West	190,000	138,000	73
Truck drivers			
Overall	162,000	97,000	60
South	132,000	86,000	65
North and West	189,000	140,000	74
Semiskilled factory workers			
Overall	167,000	120,000	72
South	143,000	97,000	68
North and West	181,000	153,000	85

Based on 1960 census figures. U.S. Senate, 88th Congress, 1st Session, *Hearings Before the Committee on Labor and Public Welfare on Bills Relating to Equal Employment Opportunities,* July and August, 1963, p. 335.

The analysis would indeed be imperfect if it were restricted to this one education group and only three occupations. The underlying census data contain similar information for about thirty different occupations. An analysis of these data produced findings very similar to those described above.

Education is not enough

Education is often prescribed as a remedy for the ills of the poor. School dropouts are urged to return. Unemployed workers are encouraged to enroll in occupational training programs. Even prisoners are given training in the hope that they can be rehabilitated. Is this prescription reasonable?

You have good reason to ask, Why train the poor—particularly the nonwhite poor? The data above show how many people have struggled to get an education only to find their skills unrewarded. The clear meaning of these figures is that education alone is not enough. More harm than good may be done if people are trained and prevented from using their newly acquired skills. It will be to no avail to train Negroes as engineers, scientists, electricians, and plumbers if the only jobs they will get are carrying the mail or working on assembly lines.

Is it wrong, then, to urge the poor, particularly the nonwhites, to get more training? Obviously not. They may be lost with training, but they are surely lost without it. It is not the desire for education or the training programs which provide it that are wrong. The trouble lies with the discrimination. Efforts to improve the economic lot of the Negro must, therefore, be carried out simultaneously and with equal force on the two fronts—education and the elimination of barriers to employment. One without the other might do more harm than good.

In 1962 the federal government stepped up its recruiting of Negroes into the middle and upper grades of civil service. During that year the number of Negroes employed in federal jobs paying $4,500 to $10,000 a year rose by 20 percent—over three times the rate of increase of all employees in these grades. This is wonderful news, but it is not enough. Real progress will come only if this rate of increase can be sustained and if large private employers can begin to make similar reports. Many of the large private firms have entered into voluntary nondiscrimination agreements with the government. It is to be hoped that before long they will be able to file the same optimistic reports that are coming from the federal government.

Who goes to college?

Since it seems clear that education is the surest road to financial success, we might take a good look at those lucky youths who get to college. Who are they? What kinds of families do they come from? How do they differ from high school graduates who don't go to college?

It has been said that in America nearly everyone goes to college. This, of course, is simply not true. It only seems that way when the United States is compared with European countries, where only a select few are permitted to get a higher education. At present, about three million American youngsters reach age eighteen each year. About two-thirds of them graduate from high school and about one-half of the graduates enter college. Thus, we have a freshman class of about one million students each year. If present trends continue, these first-year college enrollments will rise to about one and a half million by 1970. Of course, not all the entering freshmen graduate. Not by a long shot. In fact, about 25 percent drop out by the end of the freshman year and another 15 percent leave later. Only 60 percent of those who enter college leave with a sheepskin.

College students are drawn from all segments of American life. In 1960, about one-fourth of the students between twenty and twenty-four years of age came from families with incomes under $5,000, and an equal number came from families in which incomes ranged from $5,000 to $7,500; about 21 percent came from families with incomes between $7,500 and $10,000, and 29 percent from those with over $10,000. It is clear that our colleges are not rich boys' clubs. Large numbers of low-income families are represented on the campuses.

The humble origins of many college students shows up in other ways as well. Over one-third of the college students have fathers who never even graduated from high school, and the fathers of another fourth completed high school but had no college training. Thus six out of every ten college students in the United States were receiving higher education despite the fact that their fathers did not have this opportunity.

This plebeian background is further reflected in the source of support for college attendance. In 1959 the average cost to an unmarried student for one year of college was about $1,600; it's much higher at present. One out of every four college students was paying his own way entirely by his own work, savings, or a scholarship. This number was exactly equal to those whose college expenses were entirely borne by their parents. In more than half the cases the student's own work or savings contributed at least partly to his support.

Although college students are drawn from all walks of life, there can be little question that youths from higher income families are much more likely to attend college than are those brought up in families lower in the economic scale. In the fall of 1959 a national sample of high school seniors was asked about their plans to attend college. Two-thirds of the children of white-collar workers said they planned to get higher education as compared with only one-third of the children of manual workers, service workers, and farmers. Similarly, two-thirds of the children whose families had incomes of $7,500 or more said they planned to go to college. This proportion dropped progressively to 52 percent of the $5,000 to $7,500 a year families, 40 percent of the $3,000 to $5,000 a year families, and only 23 percent of the families with incomes under $3,000.

The education of the parents is a very critical factor in determining whether or not children will go to college. Indeed, the figures below show that this factor may be about as important as family income in influencing the decision of youths to get higher education.

Table VIII-8   *Percent of children attending college by education of father and family income: 1960*

Among all families	18%	Attended college
Less than $5,000	9	
Between $5,000 and $7,500	17	
Between $7,500 and $10,000	32	
$10,000 and over	44	
But if father did not graduate from high school	11	Attended college
Less than $5,000	7	
Between $5,000 and $7,500	14	
Between $7,500 and $10,000	20	
$10,000 and over	25	

Table VIII-8 (*Cont.*)

And if father attended college	51%	Attended college
Less than $5,000	23	
Between $5,000 and $7,500	37	
Between $7,500 and $10,000	66	
$10,000 and over	70	

U.S. Bureau of the Census, *Current Population Reports —Population Characteristics*, Series P-20, No. 110, Table 10.

Overall, about 18 percent of the youth were enrolled in college in October, 1960. The proportion varied considerably by income level ranging from only one child out of ten for families with incomes under $5,000 to nearly five out of ten for families with incomes over $10,000. The important point to notice, however, is that children whose fathers attended college but had low incomes were just as likely to be enrolled on a college campus as those whose fathers had high incomes but considerably less schooling. The figures show that one-fourth of the children of college men with incomes under $5,000 were attending college. This was almost identical with the proportion for men with incomes over $10,000 who did not graduate from high school. Once a man has gone to college there is a very strong probability that his children will also go to college.

How "able" are American college students? Are there many bright youths who do not attend college? These questions are difficult to answer because there are no measures of innate intelligence. It is generally conceded that results on IQ or achievement tests are influenced by cultural and emotional factors and do not in any sense measure innate qualities. Despite their limitations, however, these measures have some utility as rough indicators of the relation between ability to perform and actual performance.

The students who were in the highest quarter of their class based on their IQ scores also tended to be near the top of their class on the basis of their academic achievement, as you might expect. Similarly, those with the lowest IQ scores also tended to receive the lowest grades in their courses. Nearly all of the youths with better than average IQ scores stayed in high school at least until their senior year. Only 60 percent of the youths with below average scores got this far in school.

On the basis of either IQ or class standing there is a very high correlation between ability to perform and college attendance. About two-thirds of the brightest high school students attend college as compared with only one-third of the students in the third quarter of their class and only about one-sixth of those in the bottom fourth of their class.

However, it is significant that one-third of the brightest students do *not* attend college. This loss is serious. The young people involved almost certainly lose future income. And the nation loses the best use of its most precious resource.

CHAPTER IX

It's the job that counts

Everybody knows that bricklayers earn handsome incomes. Fantastic. And everybody knows that schoolteachers are very poorly paid. Disgraceful. Only what everybody knows isn't exactly true.

The distribution of income among occupations is full of surprises. And one of the most striking is the remarkable uniformity of reward to the average worker in nearly *all* occupations. In most jobs today, the average pay ranges between about $4,000 and $9,000 a year.

Averages can be very misleading, of course. The president of General Motors and the manager of your local A & P are both classified as "managers," yet one paycheck may be fifty times as large as the other. In many occupations, however—teaching and bricklaying are examples—such extremes of income are rare. The average figures reflect accurately the income received by the big majority of workers.

The figures for women may seem exceptionally low. This is partly due to the fact that many women work only part of the time. It is also true that many women are paid less than men for the same kind of work; but this difference can easily be exaggerated. University of Michigan Professor James Morgan and his associates report that "one economist who made crude adjustments for differences in hours worked, education, and age differences within occupations, concluded that market discrimination accounts for less than 10 percent of the difference in annual earnings of men and women."

In this discussion of occupational difference, figures

Earnings of workers in New York, Chicago, and Los Angeles

Los Angeles $5,700 $3,000

Chicago $5,600 $3,000

New York $5,100 $2,900

National average $4,600 men $2,300 women 1959

Table ix-1. *U.S. Census of Population: 1960, Detailed Characteristics, United States Summary*, Table 208 and reports for California, Illinois, and New York, Table 124.

are shown for the country as a whole and for three metropolitan areas: New York, Chicago, and Los Angeles. This will provide some measure of regional variation. One striking fact is the lower earnings of managers, skilled workers, and semiskilled workers in New York as compared to Chicago or Los Angeles. This difference is reflected in the lower average earnings for all men shown in the pictograph (Table ix-1). Women had about the same average earnings in all three areas.

The lower earnings in New York appear to reflect the lower cost of living in that city. This may come as a surprise to many New Yorkers. The cost of the budget in 1959 for a city worker family consisting of a husband, wife, and two children was $6,000 in New York, $6,300 in Los Angeles, and $6,600 in Chicago. The 10 percent differential between New York and Chicago is about equal to the difference in annual earnings. Therefore, it appears that, on the average, workers in the New York area should have been about as well off as those in Chicago, despite the earnings differential. (Earnings figures in Table IX-1 appear low relative to costs because they are for individual workers.)

The professional elite

Professional work carries the highest status in America and brings in the most money. But—because it includes such economically disparate fields as medicine and the church—the nationwide average is astonishingly low. In 1959 male professionals averaged $6,600 or about $125 a week. Geography made little real difference: $140 a week in New York, $150 in Los Angeles. Even the higher figure is not impressive considering that the average factory hand earned about $90 a week in the same year.

The physician's traditional Cadillac accurately reflects his position at the top of the heap. The best estimate that census figures give is an annual income of more than $10,000 in 1959. The data were not tabulated in sufficient detail to produce a more exact figure. Some additional information is available from unofficial sources. One survey (which probably errs on the high side) specifies $22,100 in 1959. That's the overall average for all self-employed physicians. Specialists reported much more: $34,700 for neurosurgeons.

Dentists and lawyers earn somewhat less than doctors. The census places them all in that rarefied more-than-$10,000 category. One reason for the comparatively high average of these professionals is that most of them are self-employed. They take all the risks and keep all the profits.

Technical men—engineers, scientists, architects—do quite as well as the help-wanted ads indicate (see Table IX-2). There is a marked difference between the newer specialties, which are less crowded, and the older established fields. In 1959 aeronautical engineers, for example, averaged $9,100, compared to the civil engineers' $7,700. Within each group, education and experience sharply affect income. An unofficial survey of chemical engineers in 1960 reported median salaries of about $6,000 for beginners fresh out of college, $9,000 for men with ten years' experience, and $12,000 for Ph.D.'s with ten years' experience.

For the country as a whole and in New York and Chicago, natural scientists (physicists, biologists) earned as much as social scientists (psychologists, sociologists). But in Los Angeles the natural scientists made about $1,000 a year more in 1959, reflecting perhaps the greater concentration of research industries in that area. In all areas chemists, who may be penalized by the slow growth of their profession, earned less than either group.

Teachers are not so badly off as many people think, although their overall average incomes are lower than those of any other professionals except clergymen. The worst paid are elementary school teachers. The comparatively few who are men averaged $5,200, exactly the same as skilled craftsmen and foremen. College teachers earned as much as chemists ($7,200), but there was a marked variation between the nation as a whole and the big cities. In New York college teachers earned $8,200, more than natural scientists, and in Los Angeles $8,400, a bit less than natural scientists.

The clergy is the lowest paid of all the professions. Many clergymen receive certain types of benefits, such as free living quarters, that are not reflected in their money income receipts. Even if rough allowance is made for this income received "in kind," it is very doubtful that the average earnings of clergymen even begin to approach those received in the other professions. Our spiritual leaders earn, on the average, less than truck drivers in large cities.

The figures cited above are annual earnings. The total earned over a lifetime may be more informative because it eliminates the bias introduced by unusually high or low pay for beginners. You must remember that the numbers in Table IX-3 are averages—many men make more than that and many make less. Also, the figures represent *earnings* and not total income. The difference is important for the higher paid professionals, particularly those with independent practices, who often have income from investments, rental of property, annuities, and other sources.

Doctors, of course, are by far the highest paid professionals in our society. Their expected lifetime earnings are nearly three-quarters of a million dollars on the average, which means that many go well over the one million mark.

Dentists and lawyers rank next with about $600,000 each.

Below the medical and legal professions, the range of earnings is not very wide. Electrical and mechanical engineers are in the middle brackets of the engineering profession with a little over $350,000 each; aeronautical engineers are somewhat higher paid (nearly $400,000) and civil engineers are at the bottom of that profession

Table IX-2   *Median earnings of professional men in New York, Chicago, and Los Angeles in 1959*

Occupation	National average	New York	Chicago	Los Angeles
Overall	$ 6,600	$ 7,200	$ 7,400	$ 7,700
Doctors	10,000+	10,000+	10,000+	10,000+
Dentists	10,000+	10,000+	10,000+	10,000+
Lawyers	10,000+	10,000+	10,000+	10,000+
Engineers				
Aeronautical	9,100	9,400	NA	9,600
Civil	7,700	8,300	8,300	8,600
Electrical	8,600	9,100	8,800	9,300
Mechanical	8,400	8,700	8,600	9,100
Architects	8,800	8,700	9,200	9,200
Scientists				
Natural scientists	7,700	7,500	7,800	8,900
Social scientists	7,700	7,600	7,900	7,900
Chemists	7,200	6,800	7,500	7,300
Teachers				
Elementary	5,200	6,500	5,900	6,300
Secondary	5,800	7,300	7,100	7,200
College	7,200	8,200	7,800	8,400
Clergymen	4,000	3,700	4,100	4,600

U.S. Census of Population: 1960, Detailed Characteristics, United States Summary, Table 208 and reports for New York, Illinois, and California, Table 124.

(about $335,000). Despite the variation, the range of earnings in this profession is quite narrow.

Among natural scientists, geologists are at the top with about $450,000. One of the reasons for their high earnings is that many of these men work for the large oil companies. The discovery of valuable new oil wells is primarily dependent upon their brainpower. As a result, payment for their services is high. Biologists are at the bottom of this group with $310,000. Physicists earn a little less than geologists, and chemists are only slightly better off than biologists.

The level of earnings in the social sciences is not much different from that in the natural sciences; but the teaching profession is paid at a distinctly lower scale. College professors earn about as much as the lower paid engineers and scientists; high school and elementary school teachers earn very much less.

Clergymen are by far the lowest paid among the professions shown, with only $175,000. Since this profession includes itinerant preachers, self-appointed ministers of the gospel, and others who may have had little for-

---

Table IX-3   *Lifetime earnings of professional men*

(Earnings from age 18 to 64)

Occupation	Lifetime earnings
Doctors	$717,000
Dentists	589,000
Lawyers	621,000
Engineers	
Aeronautical	395,000
Electrical	372,000
Mechanical	360,000
Civil	335,000
Natural Scientists	
Geologists	446,000
Physicists	415,000
Chemists	327,000
Biologists	310,000

Occupation	Lifetime earnings
Social Scientists	
Economists	$413,000
Psychologists	335,000
Statisticians	335,000
Teachers	
Elementary School	232,000
High School	261,000
College	324,000
Accountants	313,000
Clergymen	175,000

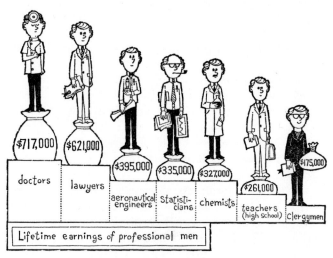

Lifetime earnings of professional men

Based on 1960 census figures. U.S. Senate, 88th Congress, 1st Session, *Hearings Before the Committee on Labor and Public Welfare on Bills Relating to Equal Employment Opportunities*, July and August, 1963, Table 1.

mal schooling or training, it is not entirely valid to compare their earnings with those of more highly trained scientists or engineers. It is significant, however, that even those clergymen who have completed five or more years of college have expected lifetime earnings of only $184,-000—considerably less than elementary school teachers and about the same as carpenters and truck drivers.

The range of earnings for professional women is much narrower than for men. For the country as a whole, professional women averaged about $3,600 in 1959 or about $70 a week. In the three metropolitan areas the average was somewhat higher, about $80 a week.

As in the case of men, the best paid jobs for women were in the medical and legal professions. Even in these occupations, however, the earnings were quite low relative to men. In the New York area, for example, women doctors averaged only $5,400 during the year. One reason for the relatively low average is the fact that a large proportion of them do not work full time throughout the year.

Women lawyers in New York had about the same average earnings as doctors, but a larger proportion worked throughout the year. Earnings among women doctors and lawyers seem to increase from east to west across the nation.

In the other professional occupations regional variations in earnings among women were quite small. High school and college teachers have similar incomes in each of the metropolitan areas. Chicago seems to pay its elementary school teachers somewhat less than the other two metropolitan areas.

Nurses and dietitians are two of the lowest paid professions among women. Both of these occupations are associated with hospitals, where wages tend to be quite low.

Table IX-4   *Median earnings of*
              professional women in 1959

Occupation	National average	New York	Chicago	Los Angeles
Overall	$3,600	$4,300	$4,200	$4,300
Doctors	5,500	5,400	6,200	7,000
Lawyers	5,200	5,400	5,900	6,100
Scientists				
Natural scientists	5,000	5,100	5,300	5,400
Social scientists	4,600	4,800	4,700	4,800
Teachers				
Elementary	4,000	5,100	4,700	5,200
Secondary	4,400	5,500	5,600	5,900
College	4,800	5,400	5,600	5,900
Librarians	3,600	4,600	4,100	4,500
Professional nurses	3,200	3,700	3,600	3,700
Dietitians	2,900	3,400	3,800	3,800

Source: Same as Table IX-2.

Salaried managers and proprietors

Managers and proprietors are America's second best-paid group. But because this classification, like the professions, includes such a miscellaneous mixture, the overall average income again is not impressive: $7,400. The managerial class takes in some of the wealthiest and most powerful men in our society—the top executives of large corporations. It also includes relatively low-paid officials in small firms. The diversity among proprietors

175

is at least as great. Business firms run the whole gamut from the itinerant TV repairman to General Electric and from the corner fruit peddler to the United Fruit Company. There are millions of small companies that have little in the way of financial assets, employ an infinitesimal part of the labor force, and obtain an even smaller share of the total sales. At the top, of course, there are the industrial giants that own most of the capital wealth, employ most of the people, and sell most of the goods. The range is enormous and the differences in returns are equally great.

One additional fact must also be borne in mind in interpreting the earnings figures for these occupations. The distinction between the owner of a business and the

Table IX-5   *Median earnings of male managers in 1959.*

Occupation	National average	New York	Chicago	Los Angeles
Salaried Managers Overall	$7,400	$8,300	$ 9,100	$8,500
Manufacturing	9,200	9,700	10,000+	9,800
Wholesale and retail trade	6,100	6,900	7,500	7,000
Finance, insurance, and real estate	8,000	8,400	9,000	8,000
Proprietors Overall	5,800	6,600	7,500	7,300
Construction	6,600	7,800	8,800	7,900
Manufacturing	8,100	9,700	10,000+	9,900
Wholesale trade	7,500	8,000	9,300	8,500
Restaurants and bars	4,900	5,500	5,700	5,800
Other retail businesses	5,200	5,600	6,300	6,400

Source: Same as Table IX-2.

manager is often just a legal fiction, particularly in the smaller firms. If a business is unincorporated, the owner-operator is classified as a proprietor. If the same business becomes a corporation, the owner-operator is called a salaried manager.

The owners and managers of manufacturing plants have higher incomes, on the average, than those in other industries. This is undoubtedly due to the fact that manufacturing firms tend to be larger and accordingly the returns are greater. The owners of wholesale businesses and managers of finance, insurance, and real estate businesses rank just below manufacturers. Lowest incomes, as might be expected, were received in restaurants and other retail stores, which are generally much smaller than the businesses mentioned above.

Clerical and sales workers

The great majority of white-collar workers are salesmen or clerks. Increases in the size and complexity of businesses have strengthened the need for management services and other office functions. The administration of advertising, research, sales, personnel, and other activities requires bookkeepers, office machine operators, secretaries. Prosperity and the increase in leisure time have also heightened the need for sales workers. As a result there have been striking increases in employment in these kinds of jobs during the past decade.

The range of responsibility, and therefore earnings, is quite narrow in most clerical jobs. Sales personnel, however, range all the way from the girl who sells nylons at Macy's to the highly trained engineer who sells computers for IBM. The former needs little if any skill; the latter must have intimate familiarity with the technical aspects of the product. The differences in training and responsibility make the range of earnings far greater for salesmen than for clerks.

Salesmen in manufacturing averaged $6,700 and retail store clerks made only $3,900. All of the other white-collar and sales jobs for men ranged between $4,400 and $6,000. Among women, the range of salaries was even narrower. Salesladies in retail stores were at the bottom with only $1,500 a year; but, of course, most of these women worked only part of the year or at a part-time job throughout the year. Cashiers earned a little more than retail sales clerks, about $2,000 during the year; but they too tend to be part-time workers. With the exception of these two jobs, the annual earnings for women in other white-collar occupations ranged only between $2,800 and $3,300.

The earnings of male clerical workers in the three large metropolitan areas were only slightly above the national average. Indeed, New York was below the national average. Salesmen in the larger cities, however, tended to be considerably above the national average. In New York and Chicago, insurance agents, and salesmen in manufacturing and wholesale trade, earn about as much as chemists.

The salaries of female white-collar workers were higher in the metropolitan areas than for the country as a whole, but the range was still quite narrow. In each of the three areas, secretaries ranked highest in the white-collar field with an average of about $4,000. Just below them were bookkeepers with earnings of about $3,700; and below them were stenographers, telephone operators, and office machine operators with earnings ranging from $3,400 to $3,800. Typists were near the bottom with $3,100 and below them were cashiers and salesladies in retail stores.

Table IX-6   *Median earnings of clerks and sales workers in 1959*

Occupation and sex	National average	New York	Chicago	Los Angeles
Men				
Overall clerical	$4,800	$4,600	$5,100	$5,100
Bookkeepers	4,400	4,600	5,200	4,900
Mail carriers	5,300	5,300	5,200	5,100
Other clerical workers	4,700	4,500	5,100	5,100
Overall salesmen	5,000	5,700	6,400	5,800
Insurance agents	6,200	6,700	6,900	6,900
Real estate agents	6,000	6,500	7,300	6,000
Manufacturing	6,700	7,500	8,100	7,400
Wholesale trade	6,000	6,700	7,200	6,700
Retail trade	3,900	4,500	5,000	4,900
Women				
Overall clerical	3,000	3,400	3,400	3,500
Bookkeepers	3,000	3,600	3,700	3,700
Cashiers	2,000	2,200	2,200	2,900
Office machine operators	3,200	3,400	3,500	3,600
Secretaries	3,300	4,000	4,100	4,000
Stenographers	3,300	3,500	3,700	3,800
Telephone operators	3,200	3,500	3,600	3,400
Typists	2,800	3,100	3,100	3,100
Retail store clerks	1,500	2,100	1,700	1,900

Source: Same as Table IX-2.

Craftsmen

One of the most durable of modern fallacies concerns the purportedly exorbitant wages paid craftsmen, particularly construction craftsmen. True, some New York City electricians get $4.96 per hour, plus $7.45 per hour for time after twenty-five hours. But their work is intermittent (for weather and business reasons). What counts is their annual income—this is what they eat and pay the rent on. It is good but not fantastic—slightly less than that of a New York elementary school teacher. Other craftsmen do not even do as well as electricians.

Although craftsmen do not have as much formal schooling as clerical and sales workers, their incomes tend to be about the same or even somewhat higher. The national average for all men classified as craftsmen or foremen was $5,200 in 1959, or exactly $100 a week. The spread around this average was not very great, with most occupations clustering around the $5,000–$6,000 mark.

Foremen are still among the highest paid in the manual field, although there are some who believe that their position is not what it once was. Their average earnings ranged from $6,000 to $7,000 for the nation as a whole, but exceeded $8,000 in some large cities.

The average earnings for the highest paid crafts in each of the trades shown centered around $6,000, or about $120 a week. The two top crafts in the building trades were electricians ($6,000) and plumbers ($5,600). In the printing trades compositors made $5,800 and other craftsmen made $6,200. Airplane mechanics, who were the top group in that field, averaged $5,900; and tool and die makers and millwrights averaged $6,500 and $6,000 respectively.

Table IX-7   *Median earnings of craftsmen in 1959*

Occupation	National average	New York	Chicago	Los Angeles
Overall	$5,200	$5,500	$6,300	$6,100
Foremen				
Manufacturing				
Durable goods	7,300	7,100	7,800	8,200
Nondurable goods	6,400	6,500	7,300	7,200
Nonmanufacturing				
industries	6,100	6,600	7,000	7,200
Construction trades				
Electricians	6,000	6,200	7,000	7,100
Plumbers	5,600	5,900	7,200	6,800
Masons	4,800	5,500	6,300	5,800
Plasterers	4,600	5,400	6,600	6,100
Carpenters	4,200	5,300	6,200	5,700
Printing trades				
Compositors	5,800	6,100	6,800	6,400
Other craftsmen	6,200	6,300	7,300	7,000
Mechanics				
Airplane	5,900	6,300	6,500	6,500
Automobile	4,300	4,800	5,600	5,400
Radio and TV	4,300	4,600	5,200	5,400
Metal trades				
Tool and die makers	6,500	6,200	7,000	6,700
Millwrights	6,000	6,600	6,500	6,600
Machinists	5,500	5,500	5,900	6,100
Structural metal				
workers	5,500	5,800	6,700	6,100
Boilermakers	5,500	5,800	6,200	5,800
Metal molders	4,800	4,800	5,300	5,000
Blacksmiths and forge-				
men	4,700	5,400	6,100	5,900

Source: Same as Table IX-2.

Most craftsmen can expect lifetime earnings ranging from nearly $200,000 to about $250,000. The range is about $50,000 lower in the South than in the rest of the country.

Electricians lead the field in the construction trades with a national average of about $250,000. They are followed closely by plumbers with about $240,000. Somewhat lower on the scale are masons and plasterers with about $210,000; and at the bottom are the carpenters with about $185,000. Differences between the earnings of whites and nonwhites in these trades are much greater in the South than in the rest of the nation. The lifetime earnings of nonwhites in the South in these trades are about 50 to 60 percent of the white total. Even in the North, nonwhites average only about 70 to 80 percent of the white total.

Airplane mechanics are about as well paid as electricians, with lifetime earnings of about $250,000. Automobile mechanics and TV repairmen, on the other hand,

---

Table IX-8   *Lifetime earnings of craftsmen*

(Numbers in thousands. Earnings from age 18 to 64)

Region and occupation	Overall	White	Nonwhite	Nonwhite as a percent of white
	UNITED STATES			
Construction trades				
Electricians	$251	$254	$189	74%
Plumbers	236	241	141	59
Masons	209	221	126	57
Plasterers	206	223	124	56
Carpenters	185	190	112	59
Mechanics				
Airplane	248	252	—	—

Table IX-8 (*Cont.*)

Region and occupation	Overall	White	Nonwhite	Nonwhite as a percent of white
Automobile	$187	$192	$132	69%
Radio and TV	183	187	—	—
	NORTH AND WEST			
Construction trades				
Electricians	261	264	—	—
Plumbers	252	255	$196	77%
Masons	229	235	163	69
Plasterers	223	232	—	—
Carpenters	209	211	164	78
Mechanics				
Airplane	257	261	—	—
Automobile	201	204	164	80
Radio and TV	194	197	—	—
	SOUTH			
Construction trades				
Electricians	223	226	—	—
Plumbers	197	207	$103	50%
Masons	168	187	107	57
Plasterers	166	196	103	53
Carpenters	139	146	81	55
Mechanics				
Airplane	231	235	—	—
Automobile	153	161	96	60
Radio and TV	159	164	—	—

Based on 1960 census figures. U.S. Senate, 88th Congress, 1st Session, *Hearings Before the Committee on Labor and Public Welfare on Bills Relating to Equal Employment Opportunities,* July and August, 1963, Table 1.

receive only as much as carpenters, who are among the lowest paid in the construction trades.

Semiskilled and service workers

Down near the bottom of the income pyramid are those men and women who perform the more routine tasks. They keep the assembly lines moving in our factories, haul the freight, bus us from one place to another, wait on us in restaurants, and perform the other services essential to urban living. For two of these service groups —policemen and firemen—earnings are on a par with those of the highest paid craftsmen. These jobs carry, of course, considerably more responsibility than most others in this category, and employment is usually obtained only after successful competition in mental and physical tests.

The other service trades for men—barbers, janitors, elevator operators, waiters, and the like—are relatively low-paying. Typical salaries range from about $60 to $80 a week (including tips). Bus drivers and truck drivers earn $100–$120 a week, but taxicab drivers make considerably less.

The variation in pay for factory work was not very great in any of the three metropolitan areas. In New York, for example, the annual earnings of semiskilled factory workers ranged from $4,000 for those employed in the manufacture of paper and paper products to $4,900 for those in food-processing plants. The range of earnings for this kind of work was about the same in Los Angeles, but even narrower in Chicago. Earnings in the traditionally low-paying laundry and dry-cleaning plants were considerably less than those paid even to the lowest paid factory workers.

Although most women are employed in white-collar jobs, large numbers also work in factories and in the serv-

Table IX-9   *Median earnings of semiskilled men in 1959*

Occupation	National average	New York	Chicago	Los Angeles
Overall semiskilled	$4,300	$4,400	$5,200	$5,100
Bus drivers	4,400	5,500	5,500	5,400
Truck drivers	4,200	5,000	5,900	5,600
Taxi drivers	3,300	4,000	3,900	3,700
Laundry and dry cleaning	2,900	3,300	3,500	3,600
Factory workers				
Chemicals	5,300	4,600	5,000	5,400
Automobiles	5,000	4,400	4,900	4,700
Paper	4,900	4,000	4,800	5,300
Machinery	4,800	4,200	5,200	5,100
Primary metals	4,800	4,600	5,100	4,900
Food	4,200	4,900	5,200	5,100
Apparel	3,800	4,400	4,600	4,300
Overall service workers	3,300	3,700	4,200	4,000
Firemen	5,500	6,100	6,100	7,000
Policemen	5,200	5,900	5,600	6,500
Barbers	3,700	3,400	4,500	4,300
Elevator operators	3,400	3,600	4,100	3,400
Waiters	3,000	3,400	3,700	3,600
Janitors	2,800	3,300	3,900	3,500

Source: Same as Table IX-2.

ice trades. Earnings in these jobs, as might be expected, are quite low. For the country as a whole, women who were semiskilled workers averaged only $2,300 in 1959, about half the amount earned by men doing the same kinds of work. The top-paying jobs were in the large manufacturing plants and the lowest paying ones were in laundry and dry-cleaning establishments. Service workers earned even less than semiskilled workers and at the

Table IX-10   *Median earnings of*
semiskilled women in 1959

Occupation	National average	New York	Chicago	Los Angeles
Overall semiskilled	$2,300	$2,400	$2,900	$2,700
Laundry and dry cleaning Factory workers	1,600	2,300	2,100	2,200
Durable goods manufacturing	2,900	2,400	3,200	3,100
Nondurable goods manufacturing	2,300	2,300	2,900	2,500
Private household workers	700	1,500	1,000	900
Overall service workers (except private household)	1,400	2,200	1,900	2,000
Charwomen	1,300	2,000	2,600	2,200
Hairdressers	2,000	2,400	2,500	2,700
Practical nurses	1,800	2,800	2,500	2,200
Waitresses	1,100	1,700	1,400	1,600

Source: Same as Table IX-2.

very bottom were domestics, who averaged only $700 in 1959.

In the large metropolitan areas, the pay in some service trades such as practical nursing and hairdressing was about on a par with factory work, and in some cases even higher. Waitresses and domestics were the lowest paid women in the metropolitan areas.

Unskilled workers

At the very bottom are those who earn their living literally by the sweat of their brows—the common laborers. These are the men who haul sticks and stones on construction projects, push things around in factories, grease cars and dent them on parking lots, and do anything that requires some brawn but little else. The low level of skill demanded is reflected in low earnings.

Longshoremen are among the highest paid workers in the unskilled group, reflecting perhaps more the strength of their union than anything else. The power of a strong union is attested by the earnings of longshoremen in Los Angeles, who make about as much as policemen and firemen and only slightly less than chemists. In the New York area, longshoremen are among the highest paid unskilled workers.

With this exception, there are few surprises in the earnings of laborers. The range is quite narrow. In the New York area the lowest paid were in the plants that manufacture machinery and the highest paid were in food processing. In Chicago there was a difference of only $300 between the lowest and highest paid laborers employed in factories.

Table IX-11   *Median earnings of unskilled men in 1959*

Occupation	National average	New York	Chicago	Los Angeles
Overall	$2,900	$4,200	$4,300	$3,700
Longshoremen	4,700	5,100	4,400	6,800
Construction laborers	3,000	4,400	4,700	4,300
Factory laborers				
Chemicals	4,000	4,200	4,500	3,600
Transportation equipment	4,200	4,300	4,400	4,200
Machinery	4,000	3,500	4,300	3,700
Primary metals	4,000	4,100	4,500	3,900
Food	3,400	4,700	4,600	3,900

Source: Same as Table IX-2.

187

CHAPTER X

Why don't you work, like other wives do?

Our affluent society would not be nearly so affluent if all married men had to support their families on what they alone make. Many people would be surprised at how far down the economic ladder single-income living would tumble them. The figures in Table x-1 are most revealing.

The column to the left shows the number of families that would be at a given income level if the family were classified by the combined income of all its members—husband, wife, children, Aunt Sophie, etc. The column to the right shows how the same families would be distributed if you counted only the husband's income. Thus, for example, if a husband made $7,000 a year and the wife made $4,000, the family would be counted at the $10,000-and-over level in the column to the left and at the $7,000–$10,000 level in the column to the right. Only families having both a husband and a wife are included in these figures and each family is counted once in each column. The great difference between the two columns reveals a great deal about where the purchasing power in many of our middle-income families comes from.

Ten thousand dollars is not a very high income by any means. One family out of six received this much money in 1961. Yet, if families were counted by the husband's income only, the number of families with in-

Table X-1	Family incomes compared to husbands' incomes in 1961	

	Families listed by:	
Income level	Family income	Husband's income
Total	40,400,000	40,400,000
Under $1,000	1,400,000	2,600,000
Between $1,000 and $3,000	5,800,000	7,700,000
Between $3,000 and $5,000	7,800,000	9,600,000
Between $5,000 and $7,000	9,300,000	10,200,000
Between $7,000 and $10,000	9,000,000	6,400,000
$10,000 and over	7,000,000	3,800,000

U.S. Bureau of the Census, *Current Population Reports —Consumer Income*, Series P-60, No. 39, Tables 3 and 26.

comes over $10,000 would be cut by almost one-half from seven million to nearly four million.

At the lower end of the distribution the change appears to be equally dramatic. An income of less than $1,000 a year to support two or more people is low no matter how you slice it. Using the family income concept, there were only about one and a half million such families in 1961. But, if only the husband's income were counted, that number would have been nearly doubled.

Evidently someone in the family is giving Dad a helping hand financially. Mother, of course. This does not mean that wives are the only family members who supplement the family incomes; but they account by far for the great majority of this income. Figures for a recent year show that supplementary earners are almost equally divided between wives and other family members, largely

21%   24%   30%   33%   34%

Under $1,000
$1,000 to $2,000
$2,000 to $3,000
$3,000 to $4,000
$4,000 to $5,000

Percent of wives who worked compared to family income:1959

sons and daughters. The wives, however, had significantly higher incomes than the other relatives, and a much larger share of it undoubtedly found its way into the family coffers.

Frederick Lewis Allen reported in *Only Yesterday* that in the early 1920's "no topic was so furiously dis-

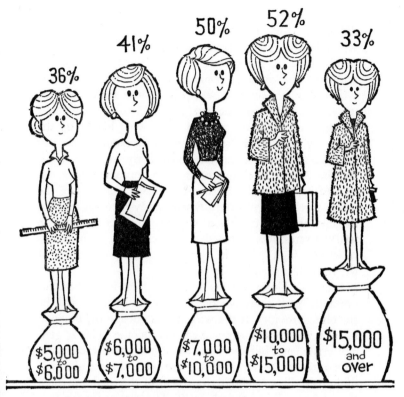

Table x-2. *U.S. Census of Population: 1960, Detailed Characteristics, United States Summary*, Table 229.

cussed at luncheon tables from one end of the country to the other as the question whether the married woman should take a job and whether the mother had a right to." This question has been resolved. Indeed, the tables have been turned and women who don't work, particularly if they have no small children at home, are often called upon to account for their failure to earn an honest living.

According to the census, four wives out of every ten did some work in 1959. These were not the poorest wives in the lowest economic groups. The *higher* the family income, the greater was the likelihood that the wife was employed. In many cases, of course, it was the wife's employment that was pushing the family income up. At the lowest income level (under $1,000) only about one-fifth of the wives worked. Somewhat higher up the scale, say among families with incomes ranging between $2,000 and $6,000, about one-third of the wives worked. At the $6,000 level the proportion increased to about two-fifths, and in the $10,000 to $15,000 class half of the wives worked. It was only when family incomes reached $15,000 or more that there was any appreciable drop in worker rates among married women. But, even at this relatively high point in the distribution, one-third of the wives had a paid job in 1959.

In the United States it is more or less taken for granted that if there is a husband in the home he will be the chief provider. If the wife works outside the home at all, she will merely supplement his income. This is generally the case, but there are some important exceptions. The 1960 census shows that there were three and a half million families, or about 10 percent of the total, in which the husband did not work at all. The reason for his failure to work is a matter for speculation. Most of these families were undoubtedly retired couples living on pensions. Others may have just been getting started and the husband was still at college. In some other cases the husband may have been disabled or he couldn't find a job. And then, of course, there are those lucky dogs who just don't want to work and manage to get by anyway. In the words of the old Irish refrain:

> I don't work for a living,
> I get along all right without.

WHY DON'T YOU WORK, LIKE OTHER WIVES DO?

I don't toil all day,
I suppose it's because I'm not built that way.
Some people work for love,
They say it's all sunshine and game.
But, if I can't get sunshine without any work
I think I'll stay out in the rain.

Who minds the store?

The picture we get for a large proportion of the families, particularly those in the middle-income brackets, is that Mama works and Papa works. Who takes care of the home and the kids? How many children are being neglected because the mother is out working? The question is a good one, but the answer is far from simple. Some authors, Michael Harrington, for one, are anything but enthusiastic about the working mother. In *The Other America* he states that the "tremendous growth in the number of working wives is an expensive way to increase income. It will be paid for in terms of the impoverishment of home life, of children who receive less care, love, and supervision." This view assumes that because Mama works she is neglecting the children. This is not necessarily the case. A very large proportion of women work only part of the year or they work at part-time jobs. This may still leave plenty of time for child care. But let us face the issue squarely and admit that many children have mothers who would rather work than stay home with them. Are we to assume that these children would necessarily be better off if their mothers stayed at home but were unhappy about it? The answer is at best debatable.

Of course, not all working wives are mothers nor are all working women wives. The figures in Table x-3 provide a good cross-section view of the characteristics of working women in 1962.

Table x-3	*Marital status of working women in 1962*		
Marital status	All women	Women workers	Percent who are workers
Age 14 and over	67,200,000	24,000,000	36%
Single	13,100,000	5,500,000	42
Married	43,800,000	14,800,000	34
Living with hus-band	41,200,000	13,500,000	33
Separated *	2,600,000	1,300,000	50
Widowed	8,400,000	2,500,000	29
Divorced	1,800,000	1,300,000	71

* Includes women whose husbands were in the armed forces or who were not living in the same household for other reasons.

Jacob Schiffman, "Marital and Family Characteristics of Workers, March, 1962," *Monthly Labor Review*, January, 1963, Table A.

About twenty-four million women were in the labor force in March, 1962; that is, they were either working or looking for work. Of these, about thirteen and a half million were married and living with their husbands. This group accounted for slightly more than half of all women workers. The remaining women workers were equally divided between those who were single and those who were widowed, divorced, or separated from their husbands.

Married women do not work as steadily as the other

groups. The economic pressure for women living with their husbands is not quite as great in most cases as it is for other women. One out of every three women living with their husbands was in the labor force in 1962. In contrast, three out of every four divorcees were working or looking for work, as were half of the women who were separated from their husbands. In both of the latter situations, the high worker rates are primarily due to the fact that most of these women are in the prime working ages, twenty-five to fifty-four years old, and they are also largely dependent upon their own work for support. Worker rates are considerably lower for single women, most of whom are under twenty years of age and still in school. Employment is also much lower among widows, who tend to be older. Slightly more than half of all widows were over sixty-five years old in 1962.

Now that we know a little bit about working women, let's see what we can discover about the children they have left behind. The figures below summarize the situation.

Table x-4   *Working women and their children in 1962*

Presence of children	Married women living with husbands		Widowed, divorced, or separated women	
	Total	Workers	Total	Workers
Total	41,200,000	13,500,000	12,800,000	5,000,000
No children under 18	17,100,000	6,200,000	10,100,000	3,500,000
Children 6 to 17 only	10,600,000	4,400,000	1,600,000	1,100,000
Children 3 to 5	4,700,000	1,300,000	400,000	200,000
Children under 3	8,800,000	1,600,000	700,000	200,000

Jacob Schiffman, "Marital and Family Characteristics of Workers, March, 1962," *Monthly Labor Review*, January, 1963, Table G.

The first thing that seems clear from these figures is that most married women who work do not have young children living with them. This was true for nearly half of the working wives and about 70 percent of the women who were widowed, divorced, or separated from their husbands. These ladies can hardly be accused of contributing to a social problem. Of course, many of the husbands may object to having their wives work, but it seems clear that their objections go unheeded.

In a recent study a sample of husbands was asked the following question: "There are many wives who have jobs these days. Do you think it is a good thing for a wife to work, or a bad thing, or what?" Only about one-third gave a favorable reply, whereas 40 percent replied unfavorably. The others were either afraid to voice an opinion or they pretended that they had none. Most of the men who liked the idea of having their wives work had their eyes on the income; but there were others who were also concerned about their mates' welfare. They felt that if their wives stayed at home they might get bored or they would not have enough to do.

There are about twelve million mothers who have school-age children at home. About five and a half million of these mothers were either working or looking for work. While there are many who feel that a large proportion of these mothers are creating social problems, there are equally strong feelings to the contrary. Most of the argument centers about the desirability of having the mother present when the child returns home from school in the afternoon. Those who object to the working mother lament the return of the child to an empty house. On the other hand, it must be recognized that a large proportion of working mothers have part-time jobs or intermittent employment and a good many of them are at home when the children return from school. But a case can even be made that the lack of a welcoming mother does not seriously deprive children. The head of the Children's Bureau, Katherine Brownell Oettinger, puts the matter this way in *Work in the Lives of Married Women:*

> More and more of us are coming to believe it is not the amount of time spent with the child but what happens during that time that really matters, so far as parent-child relations are concerned. Children who have learned to count on mother being home to greet them after school and hear what happened may feel rejected if suddenly mother is not at home. Children whose companions have mothers waiting to greet them may also feel sad if they come home to an empty house. But children for whom adequate daytime provisions are made, and who are not geared to the expectation of a waiting mother at 3:00 p.m. may adjust to being greeted and listened to at five-thirty or six o'clock. The important thing is the quality of the greeting and listening, not whether it happens two hours earlier or later. . . .

Next we come to the preschoolers between the ages of three and five. Children in this age group don't quite need the constant attention that infants require. In many cases they are eligible for nursery school. There were five million mothers of children aged three to five years. Only one and a half million of these mothers worked; the others stayed at home. About half of the separated or divorced women were in the labor market as compared with only one-fourth of the wives. The great majority of the divorcees and separatees probably had to work by any objective standards. This judgment would probably also apply to most of the wives who worked. Some of the women with young children who work, however, do so not because of economic "necessity." For example, about one-tenth of the young mothers whose husbands earned over $7,000 were in the labor market in March, 1961.

Finally, we come to the mothers with children under three years of age. In 1959 there were about eight and a half million such mothers, but only a little over one million were in the labor force. This is the age when children are most in need of a mother's care. It is quite clear that mothers of babies stay home. The great majority of those who go out to work do so out of economic necessity. About one-half of these working mothers had husbands who made less than $4,000.

Who cares for the preschool youngsters whose parents both work? A report prepared by several University of Michigan professors notes that about one-eighth of the families have a relative in the household who provides child care—generally an older brother or sister or a grandparent. In another one-sixth the children are placed in a nursery or a play school. The majority are cared for by a paid baby sitter or by a relative who does not reside with the family. About half these spending units with children under six but with all adults working did not pay anything for child care. A majority of the rest paid less than $50 a month for child care.

The kinds of work they do

Most working wives have jobs that are anything but glamorous. About two-fifths of them are salesladies or clerks. About one-sixth are employed as semiskilled factory workers, and an equal proportion work in the service trades as waitresses, hairdressers, elevator operators, etc. Altogether, about seven out of every ten working wives are employed in these four major types of jobs. Only about one out of seven holds a professional or technical job.

In view of the part-time employment and routine nature of much of this work, earnings are generally low. During the past few years, they have averaged about $1,200 a year. Those who work at full-time jobs throughout the year averaged about $3,200, or roughly $60 a week. Of course, this is gross earnings and not take-home pay. A recent study conducted by the federal government suggests that working wives may have as much as 40 percent of their earnings deducted for taxes, social security, and other expenses related to their jobs.

CHAPTER XI

A glance into the crystal ball

The Roman emperor Constantius made a law forbidding "anyone to consult a soothsayer, a mathematician, or a forecaster. . . . May curiosity to foretell the future be silenced forever." The emperor must have been a witless man to have prescribed a heavy penalty for so light a crime.

Even the penalty of death could not dampen the enthusiasm of forecasters in ancient Rome. There is surely no hope of stopping them today, nor is there any reason to do so if the figures they provide are used properly. Projections can be invaluable guides to planning if it is recognized that they are just that—guides and not blueprints. The figures in this chapter are reasonable estimates of what the future may hold in store, if the experience of the recent past does not change dramatically.

Income distribution in 1980

Barring a major disaster, the population of the United States should continue to grow during the next twenty years. Most demographers expect the rate of growth to slow down; but there is a consensus that it will continue higher than before World War II. By 1980 there should be 75 million families and unrelated individuals in the United States. That is a gain of nearly 20 million over 1960.

200

Income per family will probably increase about 2.5 percent each year. On this basis, average income will rise from $6,800 in 1960 to $11,200 in 1980, *excluding inflation.*

	1960	1980
Number of families and individuals	56 million	75 million
Aggregate income (1960 dollars)	$382 billion	$837 billion
Average income (1960 dollars)	$6,800	$11,200

The above figures show that in the next twenty years the *real* income—purchasing power—of the average family can be expected to increase by about 64 percent. What accounts for it? Explains Sidney Tickton in *Letter to a College President:* "We as a nation can achieve this great increase in income . . . because day after day we are bringing to bear on the expansion of industrial productivity all the ingenuity, the inventiveness, and the ability of our people. Further, we are concentrating more time, effort, and money on research and development on the problems of mankind than the world has ever known."

The sharp rise in average family income will be accompanied by a marked change in the distribution by income levels. In 1962, 21 percent of the families and individuals had incomes under $3,000. This number will be reduced to 12 percent by 1980. The change at the top will be equally dramatic. About 19 percent of the families and individuals had incomes above $10,000 in 1962. This proportion will rise to 30 percent by 1980. *All of these figures assume that there will be no further inflation.*

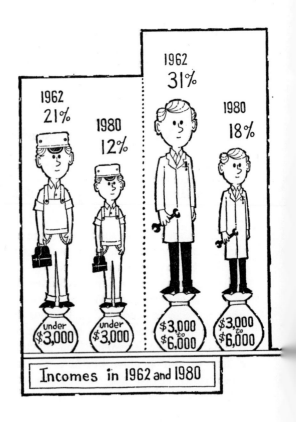

1962
21%

1980
12%

1962
31%

1980
18%

under
$3,000

under
$3,000

$3,000
to
$6,000

$3,000
to
$6,000

Incomes in 1962 and 1980

Employment patterns in 1975

Population growth and automation will produce major changes in the number of workers and the kinds of work they do. The increase in the number of workers during the sixties will be by far the largest for any ten-year period in our history. During the fifties the size of the labor force rose by eight million; the expected increase during the sixties is about twelve and a half mil-

Table xi-1. Figures for 1962 from Table iii-2. Figures for 1980 estimated by assuming a constant Lorenz curve and an annual increase of 2.5 percent in income per family.

lion—about 50 percent greater. Most of this increase will come from youth reaching working age. But it is expected that women will continue to enter the labor market in increasing numbers.

Major changes have already taken place in the composition of the labor force. These will undoubtedly continue and probably even accelerate during the next fifteen years. Farmers, unskilled, and semiskilled workers

Table xi-2   *The working population:*
1950–1975

Year	Number of workers
1950	64,700,000
1960	73,100,000
1970	85,700,000
1975	93,000,000

U.S. Department of Labor, *Manpower Report of the President,* March, 1963, Table 26.

will continue to dwindle as a proportion of the total; service workers will continue to increase as will clerks, salesmen, and professional and managerial workers. The biggest increases will take place in the occupations that require the most education and training.

Using past experience as a guide, there is every reason to believe that American workers will get the training they need. In 1960, 22 percent of the young people in the United States were attending colleges or universities either part time or full time. This proportion will rise to 34 percent by 1980. Present facilities will clearly be inadequate to train the avalanche of youth that will soon hit American colleges and universities. But we are slowly awakening to the need, and it is difficult to imagine that we will continue to neglect this crying deficiency.

There are, of course, many reasons for the changing composition of the American labor force. The following are some of the more important ones cited by the Department of Labor.

Table XI-3   *Occupations in 1960, 1970, and 1975*

Occupation	1960	1970	1975
Professional and managerial workers	22%	24%	25%
Clerical and sales	21	23	23
Craftsmen	13	13	13
Semiskilled workers	18	17	16
Service workers	13	14	14
Laborers	6	5	4
Farmers and farm workers	8	5	5

U.S. Department of Labor, *Manpower Report of the President*, March, 1963, Table 28.

Continuing shift from an agricultural economy to one that is predominantly industrial.

Rapid expansion in research and development activities.

Tremendously rapid increase in application of technological improvements.

Increasing size and complexity of business organization.

Widespread growth of record keeping among all types of enterprises.

Growing need for educational and medical services.

The problems ahead

At first glance the crystal ball promises a rather rosy outlook. The population will grow. Productivity will grow even faster. As a result, real incomes—levels of living—will rise. What then are the problems, if any, that are related to income distribution?

Two domestic problems appear to overshadow most others—unemployment and racial discrimination. Together these factors could create and perpetuate a permanently disadvantaged group in America. Although they are separate and distinct problems, they are linked together in many important ways. It is no accident that they come together at this point in our history.

So long as Negroes lived in rural southern hamlets it did not seem to matter how their lives were wasted. Even the statisticians in the Census Bureau did not count them as unemployed because they were ostensibly farming. Technological changes in farming and the lure of higher wages and presumed freedom in the northern cities took them in large numbers to the slums of the large metropolitan areas. There they were largely employed as unskilled workers or factory hands. Now once again they are being dispossessed by technological change. This time they have no place to go. Moreover, as city dwellers they have learned a most important lesson—rights must be fought for. Others will not carry on the fight for them. They now have the organization, the leadership, and the money to bring this nation to the greatest domestic crisis it has faced since the unemployment of the Great Depression. One of the underlying causes of this crisis, without a doubt, is the economic pressure brought to bear on the Negro by technological change.

The question of how to adjust employment and the distribution of output in an age of abundance has increasingly attracted the attention of political leaders and social scientists. President Kennedy has tagged this the No. 1 domestic problem in the economic field. One social scientist who has written very cogently on the subject is W. H. Ferry, Vice-President of the Fund for the Republic. Here is how he has summarized the problem in the bulletin *Caught on the Horn of Plenty:*

> The prospect is that through the 1960's the Gross National Product will continue to rise. . . . So will the total number of employed. But the likelihood is that the absolute and relative number of unemployed will also be growing as will the number of distressed areas.
>
> The question is whether jobs can be manufactured fast enough to approach full employment, using the present definition of jobs and the means of providing them that are presently regarded as acceptable. The essential contention of this paper is that the answer is no. An apparently unfavorable condition of the Age of Abundance is increasing structural unemployment and under-employment.

Viewed in this context, the relatively high level of unemployment since 1958 can hardly be regarded as a temporary situation that will be eliminated by the next turn in the business cycle or by the simple expedient of tax cuts. And the unemployed themselves can no longer be viewed as primarily unskilled and semiskilled youngsters, immigrants, Negroes, and housewives who are simply resting between engagements. According to Ferry, the ranks of the unemployed will be increasingly filled with white-collar workers and other "respectable" people who will be thrown out of work as the impact of automation is felt in the office. Indeed, he argues that "white-collar workers will after a few years comprise most of the growing category of technologically displaced."

This, of course, may be an extreme view, and many contradictory voices can be heard. For example, W. Allen Wallis, President of the University of Rochester and former Dean of the Graduate School of Business at the University of Chicago, argues that "the problem of general unemployment from automation is a nonexistent will-o'-the-wisp problem." He states further that "on the question of what actually happens in technological displacement—how many people are, as a matter of actual experience, unemployed and for how long, because of automation—there is so little factual knowledge as to be essentially none." The lack of knowledge evidently does not dampen the optimism of Dr. Wallis.

Professor John W. Kendrick, the authority on productivity, has also spoken out on this subject. He stated at the annual meeting of the National Industrial Conference Board in May, 1963, that technological change may reduce unemployment rather than raise it. "Labor," said Kendrick, "has nothing to fear from accelerated rates of technological advance." Well, maybe.

It takes only two figures to show that this is not a will-o'-the-wisp problem. Between 1947 and 1961 real output of the private economy in the United States increased by 59 percent—man hours worked rose by only 3 percent. In other words a tremendous increase in output was achieved with a slight rise in employment. How was this done? Productivity is the answer. Each hour of work today produces 50 percent more than it did fifteen years ago. As a result, we are producing more without adding appreciably to hours of work. These changes have taken place during the first fifteen years of the electronic revolution. This is only the beginning. The biggest changes are yet to come.

Unemployment is real, serious, and bound to get worse unless something is done. Like a toothache, it won't go away by pretending it is not there. Does that mean it is time to push the panic button as some have suggested? Are drastic, untried measures required to cope with this new problem? No. There is much that can and should be tried within the existing framework of our economic system before radically new measures are adopted. No single measure will suffice. But an integrated attack covering all aspects of the problem may help if it is carried out with vigor and determination.

First is the need to stimulate investment and economic growth. Without a healthy growing economy all other programs are sure to fail. Various measures have been proposed—area development assistance, liberalized depreciation regulations, tax reductions, increased government expenditures, trade expansion programs, expanded housing and urban redevelopment programs. If these are not enough, there are many other measures that can and should be tried. At every turn there are vast and unfilled needs to be met—in education, housing, health, transportation, and many other areas. All of these programs require huge investments of public and private capital. If business won't do it, the government can and will. To say that we cannot stimulate growth without trying harder than we have is to give up the fight without a struggle.

But growth is not enough. The experience of the past decade suggests that unemployment can rise despite increases in national output. If we could be sure that there was no need for additional workers in the *expanding* areas of the economy, the situation would indeed be grave and call for drastic solutions. It might then be necessary to get as many people as possible out of the labor market and guarantee them an income even though they were not currently doing "productive" work. But the evidence on this point is by no means clear or conclusive. An examination of the characteristics of the unemployed suggests that, for the most part, they lack the training to work in an electronic age. Who are the unemployed?

Workers in depressed areas.
Rural workers displaced by automation on the farm.
Negroes and other minority group workers.
Older workers.
Younger workers, particularly school dropouts.
Unskilled workers.
Displaced skilled and semiskilled workers who need retraining.

For some of these workers it is already too late. The best that can be done is to retire them with as much dignity and income maintenance as is possible under the circumstances. For most of them, however—and for their children—there is much that can and should be done. They cannot be fully employed as they are or where they are. With training, however, and incentives to move, their services may again be in great demand in the expanding industries or in new industries that have not yet come into existence.

The outline of an active labor market program to deal with this problem now exists on paper. At present it is only a token program. But it is a beginning and it could become a real program if it gets support and drive at the grass roots level. Here it is as summarized before a Congressional committee by the Under Secretary of Labor:

1. An up-to-date current labor market information service for workers and employers, assessing and communicating the results of such information as job vacancies, occupational needs, availability of workers and skills at all the critical junctures where this type of information counts—particularly in a systematic manner at all placement services.

2. An early warning system of impending changes, especially layoffs, again communicated to where it counts, e.g., the employment services, so that preventive work can be immediately initiated to place in jobs or put into training those who are scheduled to be displaced. Similarly, early expansion would facilitate efficient manning and growth.

3. An effective informational service for career guidance and counseling before entry into working life and, of course, an effective system of guidance activities beginning at the elementary school level (the latter especially important in view of the school dropout problem) and continuing throughout a person's working life.

4. A corresponding educational system, vocational as well as academic, which is responsive to current and upcoming manpower needs.

5. An expanded apprenticeship training program.

6. A well-endowed system of placement services which focuses not only on a given labor market but is national in scope.

7. A program of training and retraining for unemployed and underemployed workers, as well as a program for equipping employed skilled workers with additional skills to meet increasing technical demands.

8. A program for aiding the mobility of workers, responsive to the changing geography of employment opportunities.

9. The elimination of racial discrimination in employment, training, and education.

Will the Negro's lot improve?

On this question the image in the crystal ball grows dim indeed. Many factors are involved. So long as large numbers of Negroes remain in the South it is difficult to see how their lot can improve very much. In the first place, southern states with large concentrations of Negroes have very low per capita incomes. Mississippi, for example, with 900,000 Negroes is in fiftieth position—at the very bottom—in a ranking of states by per capita income; South Carolina with 800,000 is in forty-ninth place; Arkansas with 400,000 is in forty-eighth place; Alabama with 1,000,000 is in forty-seventh place; etc. So long as the Negro continues to live in these states he is bound to be the low man on a short totem pole. But even if conditions improve in this region, the Negro may still be in great trouble. It is one thing to get a student or two admitted to a university or to get the right to drink a cup of coffee at a lunch counter and quite another to get a decent chance at a good job or an education. Racial discrimination in the South is not just an American idiosyncrasy; it is a social disease that has been festering for 250 years. Relationships of such long standing are not likely to change radically in 20 years.

Nobody knows if future Negro migration from the South will be more or less rapid than it has been in the past. Some numbers in current circulation seem to exaggerate the rate at which the Negro will leave the South. One article states: "By 1975, it is predicted, 85 percent of all Negroes—instead of the current 50 percent

—will live in northern urban centers." Such estimates tend to ignore the fact that getting Negroes out of the South is like trying to empty a bathtub with the faucets turned on full blast. Many Negroes are leaving the South, but those who remain have very high birth rates. As a result, there is a constant replacement of population despite the high rate of emigration.

The numbers in Table xi-4 show the proportion of Negroes who will still be living in the South in 1980, based on more-or-less realistic assumptions. The specific method used to make this projection was to assume that the average annual rate of change in the ratio of Negro to total population in the South during 1940–60 would decline linearly to zero between 1960 and 1985. In other words it was assumed that the ratio of Negro to total

Table xi-4   *Negroes living in the South: 1940–1980*

Year	Negroes in South * as percent of all Negroes
1940	72%
1950	63
1960	54
1970	46
1980	42

* The "South" refers to the census South region excluding Washington, D.C., Maryland, Delaware, and West Virginia.

1940–60 from U.S. Bureau of the Census, *Statistical Abstract of the United States, 1962*, P. 30. 1970–80 estimated by the author.

213

population in the South would keep decreasing until 1985, at which time stability would be attained. If these assumptions are valid, two out of every five Negroes will still be in the South by 1980.

Movement from the South by itself would not be enough to improve the economic lot of the Negro appreciably. At least two other things are required: the elimination of discrimination in employment, housing, and education in the North; and a change in Negro family life which is not now conducive to economic growth. The first of these points is obviously critical. So long as the Negro is not given a chance, he will not do well. Much has been written on this subject and there is no need to repeat it here. There can be no doubt that there will be a reduction in discrimination during the next twenty years and that the economic position of many Negroes will improve as a result.

Even if discrimination were eliminated completely, a large proportion of Negroes would still be disadvantaged economically because of the instability of their family life. One out of every five Negro children grows up in a fatherless home as compared with about one out of twenty white children. These children not only grow up deprived of the love and care of a father, but also lacking many economic advantages because their mothers cannot get good jobs. In some cases mothers' jobs would be improved if discrimination were ended. In most cases, however, it would probably not make much difference. If they keep having children at an age when they should still be in school, they will continue to doom themselves and their children to lives of hardship.

APPENDIX

The validity of
income statistics

Most of the income figures in this book come from either the decennial census or the annual sample surveys of income conducted by the Bureau of the Census. In order to appraise these figures, it is necessary to understand how censuses and sample surveys are conducted.

The principal source of population data in the United States is the Decennial Census of Population, a house-to-house enumeration made every ten years. The first census was taken in 1790 in accordance with a constitutional provision for a population count every decade. The primary purpose of the Census of Population, as set forth in the Constitution, is to provide a basis for the apportionment of members of the House of Representatives among the several states. It was very soon recognized that much more information than a simple count of persons by age and sex was needed and that it could be obtained by enumerators while they were in the household. So additional questions were added to the census schedule very early in our history.

In 1940, income questions were asked in response to demands for data that might throw light on the causes and impact of the depression of the thirties. Despite the long experience with the collection of financial data, some objections were anticipated. For this reason, the questions were kept simple. Each person was asked to report only the amount of wages or salaries received during 1939 and whether he received $50 or more of nonwage income. Specific questions about the amount of nonwage income received were not asked for fear of antagonizing some respondents. To further minimize resistance, respondents were not asked to report the exact amount of wage income if it was above $5,000, and confidential forms were provided for those respondents who did not wish to report their information to local enumerators (who might also be neighbors).

The cooperation of the public was excellent. Only 2 percent of the wage and salary workers failed to report their income and only 200,000 people bothered to use the confidential forms (15 million forms had been printed). An appraisal of these data that was published by the National Bureau of Economic Research stated that although "the amount of wages and salaries was somewhat underreported . . . the 1939 statistics were reasonably accurate and they provided a wealth of data on income."

Following the success of the 1940 census and the widespread use made of the income data that were collected, there were strong demands for the inclusion of income questions in the 1950 census. These demands came from many different sources: business groups, labor unions, government agencies, research organizations, universities, and many others. The demand this time was for total income and not just wages, partly because the wage data were unduly restrictive, but also because it had been demonstrated in numerous sample surveys that respondents would willingly provide detailed information on sources of income.

Income questions included in the 1950 census were quite different from those used in 1940. In the first place, the scope was expanded to include all types of income and not just wages and salaries. A second change involved the movement of the income questions from a 100 percent basis to a 20 percent sample. Every fifth line on the 1950 census questionnaire was marked "sample line." The person enumerated on that line was asked a special set of sample questions. In the case of income he was asked to report the amount received during 1949 from wages and salaries, self-employment, and income other than earnings. If the sample person was a family head, the same questions were repeated for other family members as a group. The enumerator had no control in the selection of the "sample lines" because persons had to be listed in a prescribed order on the census questionnaire.

The shift in the income questions to a sample basis did not represent a downgrading in the importance of this item nor did it reduce the quality of the statistics. On the contrary, the income questions were considered very important and it was felt that the shift to a sample might improve the accuracy of the data because the money saved by reducing the cost of enumeration could be used to provide better training for the enumerators. The reasoning behind the change of the income questions to a sample basis in 1950 has been explained as follows: "The income questions were moved from 100 percent to 20 percent coverage . . . as a part of the historical development of census taking. The uses of the statistics for these items did not require 100 percent enumeration, and money and time were saved by putting the items on a sample basis. The sample was still a very large one compared to those used to collect annual data and it provided usable income information for relatively small areas."

Public cooperation in the 1950 census was, once again, very good. Complete income information was obtained from 93 percent of the persons of whom the questions were asked. A special study that was made of non-respondents showed that their incomes did not differ appreciably from those who reported.

In 1960 the sample was expanded to 25 percent. The same income questions were used as in 1950, but there were some important changes in procedures. In the first place, the sample was changed to a household basis instead of a line basis. This change had important implications for the quality of the income data. It meant that in 1960 every fourth household, selected at random, was in the sample and income questions were asked individually for each member of the household. In 1950, every fifth *person* was in the sample, and if he was a household head income questions were asked for him and for all his relatives in the household *as a group*. The use of separate income questions for each family member in 1960 considerably improved the quality of the family income statistics.

Another important change introduced in 1960 was the advance distribution of forms and the use of self-enumeration. The 1960 census was the first in which self-enumeration was used. A questionnaire, entitled "Advance Census Report," was mailed to every household in the country. This questionnaire contained the complete count (100 percent) information collected in the census: name, address, age, sex, color, marital status, and household relationship. The instructions on the ACR requested that one or more members enter on the form the answers to all questions for each person in the household. The enumerator was instructed to correct omissions and obviously wrong entries by asking the necessary questions. In sparsely populated areas (with 65 percent of the land area and 18 percent of the population), the enumerator collected the complete-count information and also asked the sample questions at the time of his visit. In the rest of the United States, where most of the population lives, the enumerator collected the complete-count information and also left with each sample household a Household Questionnaire, containing the sample questions to be answered. Income was one of these sample items. The respondents were requested to complete these questionnaires and mail them to the local census offices. Where this was not done, or where the schedules were incomplete, follow-up visits were made to collect the missing information.

The Current Population Survey

The income data from the decennial censuses are primarily designed to provide figures for geographic areas like cities, towns, and census tracts or for small groups in the population for which data cannot be obtained from other sources. For example, if you wanted to know how much carpenters make a year in Pittsburgh or how many elderly couples with incomes under $1,000 were living in substandard housing in Chicago, you almost certainly would have to take a census or a very large sample. Although sampling was used to collect the census income data, the samples were very large and they provide figures that vary only slightly from the information that would be obtained from a complete count. Of course, even a 25 percent sample would be too small to produce reliable figures for individual city blocks or for other very small areas; but for most purposes it is more than adequate.

Conducting a census is a very expensive undertaking and it is done only once every ten years. Between censuses there is need for nationwide information to show major trends and to help formulate national policy. For example, we might want to know each year how many elderly couples in the country as a whole live in substandard housing; or we might want to know how the composition of the bottom or top income groups has changed. This type of information does not require a census. It can be obtained from a relatively small sample survey. That is the function of the Current Population Survey (CPS) conducted by the Bureau of the Census. The size and design of CPS have been changed several times during the twenty years it has been in operation. The following is a description of the survey in mid-1963.

CPS is a nationwide survey, covering about 35,000 interviewed households widely distributed throughout the fifty states and the District of Columbia. It provides monthly data on employment and unemployment. Once each year, in March, information on annual income is also collected from three-fourths of the entire sample.

The CPS is a scientifically designed, carefully controlled sample. A complete description of the procedures used to design the sample and insure the accuracy of the results appears in the Census Bureau report, *The Current Population Survey: A Report on Methodology*, Technical Paper No. 7. What follows is a condensed summary taken from this paper and from the report of the International Labor Office, *Family Living Studies*.

The Washington office staff directly concerned with CPS is relatively small, consisting of eight to ten statisticians and a clerical force of about fifteen people; others are added at peak periods each month to meet a rapid time schedule. The statisticians are assisted by specialists from other parts of the Census Bureau and from other federal agencies. They are responsible for the definitions used, the preparation of questionnaires and instructions, determination of sample design and estimation techniques, the planning of processing and tabulation procedures, and the review and analysis of the results.

The field work is conducted through twelve regional offices. Each office is directed by a regional supervisor who has several assistants. They supervise a total of about 650 part-time enumerators and are responsible for their selection and training, review of their work each month, and periodic field checks and direct observation. Detailed instructions are provided by the Washington staff on selection of sample areas, training procedures, and review of work. The enumerators are mostly women who work part time. All of them must pass written tests of their ability to read maps and to absorb written instructions.

The heart of CPS is, of course, the sample. If that is wrong, nothing else can be right except by chance. The number of areas covered and the number of interviews conducted in each area depends primarily on the size of the sampling error that can be tolerated and the total amount of money available for the survey. One of the key determinants of the nature and design of the CPS sample is the fact that Congress authorizes an annual budget of about $2 million for the survey. The second major determinant is the fact that the survey is intended to measure an unemployment level of 2,500,000 with a standard error of 75,000. This means that the sample must be designed in such a way that when unemployment is 2,500,000 the chances should be 19 out of 20 that a full census would not produce results outside of the range 2,350,000 and 2,650,000, i.e., within a band of two standard errors above and below the figure provided by the sample. Given the cost and the desired level of reliability, it was determined that about 35,000 households could be interviewed in 357 primary sampling units.

The actual mechanics for the selection of the sample are described in the Census Bureau report referred to previously (Technical Paper No. 7). The basic procedure involves the grouping of the 3,103 counties and independent cities of the United States into about 1,900 primary sampling units (PSU) consisting usually of a county or a group of contiguous counties. The 107 largest standard metropolitan statistical areas are automatically included in the sample as are five other special cases. All of the other PSU's are classified into 245 groups and one PSU is selected in a random manner to represent its group.

The selection of individual households within each PSU for enumeration each month is made in the following way. The PSU is divided into enumeration districts, each containing about 800 people. (These same enumeration districts were assignments for individual enumerators in the 1960 census.) A sample of enumeration districts is then selected with probability proportionate to its population size in 1960. The selected districts are then divided into segments or clusters which contain an average of about six dwellings units or other living quarters. For the nation as a whole, about 6,000 segments are in the sample in any given month. The enumerators visit these segments and interview the people living there.

Reliability of the figures— sampling error

Since the income figures collected by the Bureau of the Census are based on samples, they differ somewhat from the figures that would have been obtained from a complete census using the same questionnaires, instructions, and enumerators. The measure of the variation due to sampling is called the standard error. It shows the variations that occur *by chance* because a sample rather than the entire population is used. Table a-1 shows the standard errors for selected characteristics based on the 25 percent sample used in the 1960 Census and the Current Population Survey. The chances are two out of three that an estimate from the sample would differ from a complete census figure by less than the standard error.

As you can see from the figures in the table, the sampling variability of the 1960 census figures is so small that it can be ignored for large areas or for major groups. This is because of the very large size of the sample. The CPS figures are subject to much wider sampling variations because this is a sample of 1 in about 1,500 as compared with 1 in 4 used in the census. But, even the variations for CPS are relatively small for those characteristics that are based on a large number of persons or families. For example, the average (median) income of all families in the March, 1960, CPS was $5,417. The standard error of this estimate was only $38. This means that, had a complete census been taken using the questionnaire, training, and enumerators used in CPS, the chances are two out of three that the median would have been within the range of $5,379-$5,455. For other characteristics, like the median income for nonwhite individuals, the relative sampling error is considerably larger; but even here it is small enough to provide usable figures for many characteristics at the national level.

Errors in response and nonreporting are potentially more serious than sampling errors. In fact, these are the kinds of errors most people have in mind when they speak of the shortcomings of census income data. They are discussed in some detail below.

Table A-1   *Standard error of median income: Census vs. Current Population Survey*

Characteristics	1960 Census		March, 1960, CPS	
	Median income	Standard error	Median income	Standard error
Families				
Overall	$5,660	$ 0	$5,417	$ 38
White	5,893	0	5,643	24
Nonwhite	3,161	0	2,917	95
Unrelated individuals				
Overall	1,596	0	1,556	55
White	1,654	0	1,663	70
Nonwhite	1,217	0	1,075	116
Male professional workers				
United States	6,619	0	6,725	122
Chicago Metropolitan Area	7,385	40	—	—
Male managerial workers				
United States	6,664	0	6,315	130
Chicago Metropolitan Area	8,474	58	—	—
Male nonfarm laborers				
United States	2,948	0	3,150	107
Chicago Metropolitan Area	4,259	65	—	—
Female professional workers				
United States	3,625	0	3,603	127
Chicago Metropolitan Area	4,153	85	—	—

Computed from figures shown in *U.S. Census of Population: 1960, General Social and Economic Characteristics, United States Summary;* and *Current Population Reports—Consumer Income*, Series P-60, No. 35.

Accuracy of the figures

Sampling errors in census income statistics can virtually be ignored when major national totals are being considered. The same generalization cannot be made with respect to the *accuracy* of the figures because major errors can and do arise from nonresponse and poor reporting. Unlike sampling errors, which are computed according to standard and generally accepted statistical procedures, there are no such procedures for measuring the accuracy of a survey. Evaluations must be prepared separately for each type of statistic, and their acceptance depends largely on judgments regarding the reliability of the figures used as benchmarks.

One of the outstanding innovations introduced in the 1950 Census of Population and Housing was an intensive effort to evaluate the statistics that were collected. A carefully designed reinterview survey was conducted, record checks were made, and numerous other studies were undertaken for the purpose of measuring the quality of the data and discovering methods of improving future censuses and household surveys. These studies led to major changes in the methods used in the 1960 censuses and there is general agreement that for most subjects, including income, the 1960 data are more accurate than those collected ten years earlier. The evaluation effort, started in 1950, was intensified in 1960. The following are brief descriptions of the major sources of data that were used to evaluate the income statistics. Wherever possible 1960 census figures are shown; in some cases, however, only 1950 figures were published.

a. *Office of Business Economics* (OBE) *estimates*. The Office of Business Economics of the Department of Commerce prepares annual estimates of gross national product, national income, and other related measures that comprise the national income accounts. Primary emphasis in this series is placed on aggregates which have been published annually since the early forties and are generally ranked among the most important and most accurate of all statistical series prepared by the federal government.

Most projects in the census evaluation program in 1950 and 1960 required the collection of additional data with which the original census results could be compared or which would in other ways throw light on possible biases or other shortcomings in the data. The OBE estimates, however, provided an excellent benchmark against which the census results could be compared. At relatively little expense, the published figures were recast by OBE on a directly comparable basis with the census figures.

b. *Current Population Survey* (CPS). In 1950 and 1960 persons who were asked about income in the March CPS were also asked to report income information in April in the decennial census. Comparisons of the answers, called a CPS-census matching study, provide two different measures of income for the same year for each person, collected on the average about one month apart.

c. *Reinterview Surveys.* Several months after the completion of the field work in the 1950 and 1960 censuses, households that had been asked about income were reinterviewed. The purpose of the reinterview survey was to provide a quality check of the information originally obtained in the censuses. Therefore, the enumerators were specially selected, paid premium rates, and given intensive training by members of the Washington staff in the use of a very detailed questionnaire.

d. *Tax returns.* In 1950 and 1960 an attempt was made to compare the income data obtained in the census for given individuals with comparable information available on tax returns of the Internal Revenue Service. In 1950, a sample of census returns was selected and an attempt was then made to locate the records for that sample in the files of IRS. A relatively large proportion of the records could not be found. In 1960, the procedure was reversed and a sample of tax returns was first selected and then matched with census returns.

Comparison of Census and Office of Business Economics aggregates

The aggregate income estimates published by the Office of Business Economics of the Department of Commerce are the most comprehensive income figures published by the federal government. They are based largely on data derived from business and governmental sources, including industrial and population censuses, employees' wage reports under the social security program, and records of disbursements to individuals by governmental agencies. Because of the great care and effort that goes into the compilation of these data, they hold a unique position as a cornerstone of the statistical program of the federal government. These data provide an excellent benchmark for the evaluation of the income figures collected in the decennial censuses and the annual household surveys.

The census and OBE aggregates are not directly comparable in the form in which they are published. The census figures represent total money income, which is defined as the sum of money wages and salaries, net income from self-employment, and income other than earnings. More detailed classifications within each of these types of income were not collected in the decennial censuses. The "unearned" income category includes social security, veterans' payments and other government or private pensions; interest, dividends, and income from annuities, estates, or trusts; net income from boarders or lodgers or from renting property to others; and other types of income including unemployment or sickness benefits, public assistance, alimony, military dependency allotments, and other periodic income other than earnings.

The OBE estimates of personal income are prepared in great detail with respect to income classification and they can be adjusted by adding and subtracting components so as to be made conceptually comparable with the money income figures described above.

A comparison of census and OBE estimates of aggregate income by type of income is shown for 1949 and 1959 in the table below. CPS data for the same years are also shown in this table to provide a general background against which the overall census results may be compared.

In 1949, the census aggregates represented 91 percent of the OBE estimate and in 1959 this proportion was increased to 94 percent. In both years CPS obtained a smaller percent of the aggregate, 84 percent in 1949 and 87 percent in 1959.

A comparison of the census and OBE estimates by type of income shows that in 1949 and 1959 there was very close agreement for wages and salaries but evidence of substantial underreporting of income other than earnings in the census. The census wage and salary aggregate amounted to 99 percent of the OBE estimate in 1959 and

Table A-2   *Aggregate income in 1949
and 1959: Office of Business
Economics—Census—
Current Population Survey*

(Dollar figures are in billions)

Year and type of income	OBE	Census	CPS	Census as % of OBE	CPS as % of OBE
1949					
Overall income	$191.0	$173.2	$159.8	91	84
Wages and salaries	128.8	124.3	120.0	97	93
Self-employment	31.3	31.1	26.5	99	85
Income other than earnings	30.9	16.6	13.3	54	43
1959					
Overall income	351.4	331.7	306.7	94	87
Wages and salaries	249.1	246.5	233.5	99	94
Self-employment	42.2	47.9	38.3	114	91
Income other than earnings	60.1	37.3	32.7	62	54

Conrad Taeuber and Morris H. Hansen, "A Preliminary Evaluation of the 1960 Census of Population," paper presented at the April, 1963, meetings of the Population Association of America.

97 percent in 1949. The census estimate of income other than earnings, on the other hand, amounted to only 62 percent of the OBE estimate in 1959 and 53 percent in 1949. In each case the census estimate was in closer agreement with OBE than were the CPS figures. There was also substantial reduction in underreporting from one census to the next.

Comparison of CPS and Census

Essentially two types of comparisons can be made between the income data collected in CPS and in the census: (a) distributions or averages can be compared for many different characteristics like age, sex, color, education, etc.; and (b) tabulations can be made for an identical sample of persons who provided information in both surveys.

Overall comparisons of distributions and averages reveal net differences between the two surveys but they provide little insight into the reasons for these differences. Moreover, comparisons of this type do not provide a validation of either set of statistics since neither one can be regarded as a suitable benchmark. Despite these limitations, there is understandable interest in comparing the results of these two surveys since they both attempt to measure the same thing. In addition, the CPS income surveys have provided meaningful and useful income statistics for nearly twenty years, and to this extent, at least, they provide a reasonable base against which the census results can be compared.

The second type of comparison, generally referred to as a CPS-census match, involves the analysis of reports obtained for an identical sample of persons who were included in both CPS and the census. Persons who were interviewed in the CPS in March, 1960, were also included in the decennial census sample and were asked to provide income information. A similar study was made in 1950. As might be expected, a large proportion of the respondents did not report the same figures in both surveys. The CPS-census match provides a vehicle for measuring the extent of response variation and its likely impact on selected cross-classifications of income and other variables. This study provides a basis for getting behind the net errors detected in overall distributions and discovering some of the reasons for the differences. To the extent that nonrespondents in one survey were interviewed in the other, the CPS-census match also sheds light on possible biases introduced into each set of data due to nonresponse.

In 1949 and 1959 the census estimates tended to exceed CPS. For all males and for white males the differences amounted to about $100 in both years; for nonwhites the absolute and relative differences were considerably greater, amounting to $150 in 1949 and $300 in 1959. The latter figure represents a 15 percent differential between the two estimates. For females, both white and nonwhite, the census estimates tended to exceed CPS by about $100 in 1949 and 1959 (see Table II-1).

The estimates cited above are for the country as a whole. For male and female nonfarm residents the differences in both years were so small as to be insignificant. In contrast, the census medians for male farm residents in both years were about one-fourth higher than CPS and for females the 1959 median was also substantially higher than CPS. It is possible that the farm income figures are overstated in the census because of a tendency to report gross income from farm operations rather than net income.

About one-fourth of the persons who were in the March, 1960, income supplement to CPS were asked to report income information in the 1960 census. Similarly, about one-fifth of the persons in the March, 1950, income supplement were asked to report on income in the 1950 census. Upon completion of each census, an attempt was made to match the reports obtained for identical persons in CPS and the census using name, address, age, sex, color, and other means of identification. In 1960, census records were found for about 93 percent of the persons who were in the CPS income sample. After the records were matched a comparison was made of the amount of income reported in each survey. The results of such a comparison with respect to total money income are summarized in Table A-3. The income concept and period covered by both surveys were the same. Therefore, variations in the responses are not due to conceptual differences but rather to a variety of other factors. In 1950 these included differences in the quality of the enumerators, and variability of response due to such things as the memory factor and change in respondents. In addition to the factors noted above, differences for 1960 could be

Table A-3   *Consistency of income reporting to Current Population Survey and Census in 1950 and 1960*

Comparison of CPS and census	Male		Female	
	1960	1950	1960	1950
Persons reporting on income in CPS and census:				
Percent in same income class in both	56%	62%	73%	77%
Percent in higher income class in CPS	20	21	14	13

Table A-3 (*Cont.*)

Comparison of CPS and census	Male		Female	
	1960	1950	1960	1950
Percent in higher income class in census	24%	18%	13%	11%
Of all persons reporting no income in CPS: Percent with income in census	26	43	12	12
Of all persons reporting no income in census: Percent with income in CPS	34	38	14	14
Median income: CPS	$4,327	$2,514	$1,508	$1,152
Census	4,406	2,444	1,524	1,163
Nonrespondents in CPS: Percent reporting in census	90	75	92	85
Median income in census	$4,862	$3,095	$2,491	$1,000
Nonrespondents in census: Percent reporting in CPS	88	88	94	92
Median income in CPS	$3,216	$2,373	$1,093	$1,000

Unpublished data of the Bureau of the Census.

due to the use of self-enumeration in the census as compared with direct enumeration in CPS.

Table A-3 shows that there are considerable variations in the reports received for identical persons in each survey; however, these variations tended to cancel each other, leaving the overall distributions unchanged. This was true for both males and females in both censuses. This table shows no significant differences in the medians, the distributions by income levels, or the proportions of income recipients.

Comparison of Census and Reinterview Survey results

Upon completion of the field work in the 1950 and 1960 censuses, intensive Reinterview Surveys (RES) were conducted to detect possible biases in the census results. In 1950, about 25,000 households were reinterviewed but income information was obtained only for about 5,000 households that were in the 20 percent sample. These results have been published (see Bureau of the Census, *The Post-Enumeration Survey: 1950*). In 1960, the RES sample consisted of about 3,400 households that were included in the 25 percent census sample. These results were not published at the time of this writing.

The RES is intended to serve as a benchmark against which the census results can be compared. For this reason, the special measures described below were incorporated in RES to insure that the most accurate results were obtained. Partly because of these measures field cost per person in the 1950 RES was about twenty times that in the census.

a. The income information was obtained whenever possible from the person himself (in the census, information for all household members was obtained from any responsible member of the household).

b. RES used detailed "probing" questions in contrast to the more general questions used in the census.

c. Superior interviewers were selected and given more intensive training and closer supervision than was possible in the census.

d. The RES and census information was compared case by case and attempts were made to reconcile discrepancies in the field.

Despite these efforts to obtain the most accurate answers, the RES results have several shortcomings. In the first place, the accuracy of the information depends on how well the interviewers did their job, on the adequacy of the information provided by the respondents, and on their willingness to cooperate. In addition, the effectiveness of RES as an evaluation of the censuses is reduced by the length of the interval between the two surveys. In 1950, most of the field work was not done until August or September, or about four or five months after the completion of the census and eight or nine months after the end of the calendar year to which the income data pertained. In 1960, 1,400 households in RES were interviewed in July, but the remaining 2,000 were not interviewed until October, 1960.

In general, the 1950 data suggest that the major difference between RES and census was that RES found a relatively large number of persons with small amounts of income who reported no income in the census. For persons who reported $1 or more of income in both surveys, the overall results were very similar despite considerable variability of response.

Table A-4 shows that about 20 percent of the men without income in RES reported income in the census; but proportionately twice as many who reported no income in the census were found to have income in RES. This difference is considerably greater than that noted earlier for the CPS-census matching study and is probably due to the more intensive questioning used in RES. For men who reported income in both surveys, however, the medians were about $2,500 in each survey and the differences by income level were very small. In the aggregate, therefore, the RES results do not differ substantially from those obtained in the census.

Table A-4 also shows that variability of response in the 1950 RES-census matching study was very similar to that obtained in the CPS-census matching study. About 60 percent of the men were in the same income interval in RES and the census, 24 percent were in a higher RES interval and 16 percent were in a higher census interval.

Table A-4	Consistency of income reporting to Reinterview Survey and Census in 1950	
Comparison of RES and census	Male	Female
Persons reporting on income in RES and census:		
Percent in same income class in both	61%	76%
Percent in higher income class in RES	24	16
Percent in higher income class in census	16	8

Table A-4 (*Cont.*)

Comparison of RES and census	Male	Female
Of all persons reporting no income in RES:		
Percent with income in census	18%	8%
Of all persons reporting no income in census:		
Percent with income in RES	39	17
Median income:		
All persons		
RES	$2,580	$1,140
Census	2,520	1,080
White		
RES	2,700	1,250
Census	2,640	1,190
Nonwhite		
RES	1,430	680
Census	1,320	620

Leon Pritzker and Alfred Sands, "The 1950 Census and the Post-Enumeration Survey," *Studies in Income and Wealth*, Vol. 23, Princeton University Press, 1958, p. 221.

Source Notes

(The numbers on the left refer to the pages on which the data and quotations appear.)

1 *The New York Times*, November 11, 1962.

2 Paul A. Samuelson, *Economics: An Introductory Analysis*, 5th ed. New York, McGraw-Hill Book Co., Inc., 1961, p. 113.

3 Facts cited for unrelated individuals are from U.S. Bureau of the Census, *How Our Income Is Divided*, Graphic Pamphlet No. 2, 1963.

6 Henry Wallich, *The Cost of Freedom*. New York, Harper & Row, Publishers, 1960, p. 114.

6 C. Wright Mills, *The Power Elite*. New York, Oxford University Press, 1956 (Galaxy Books, 1959, p. 149).

6 The 1959 tax figures for persons with incomes above $100,000 are from U.S. Bureau of the Census, *Statistical Abstract of the United States: 1962*, p. 392.

7 The 1959 figures for high incomes in New York, Chicago, and Los Angeles are from Internal Revenue Service, *Statistics of Income: Individual Income Tax Returns for 1959*, Table 19.

8 Charles Péguy, *Basic Verities*. New York, Pantheon Books, 1943, p. 61.

8 Lincoln's statement was a reply to the New York Workingmen's Democratic Republican Association, March 21, 1864. It is quoted in *The Collected Works of Abraham Lincoln*, Vol. 7, ed. by Roy P. Basler. New Brunswick, N.J., Rutgers University Press, 1953, p. 259.

8 R. H. Tawney, *Equality*. New York, G. P. Putnam's Sons (Capricorn Books), 1961, p. 40.

10 For additional comparisons between the United States and other countries, see Leonore Epstein, "Unmet Need in a Land of Abundance," *Social Security Bulletin*, May, 1963.

11 Aldous Huxley, *Ends and Means*. New York, Harper & Row, Publishers, 1937, p. 187.

11 For Max Eastman's ideas, see the above source.

11 United Nations, Economic and Social Council, *Statistics of Income Distribution*, E/CN.3/184, January, 1954, p. 6.

11 Simon Kuznets, "Quantitative Aspects of the Economic Growth of Nations," *Economic Development and Cultural Change*, Vol. XI, January, 1963, p. 12.

14 Clarence B. Randall, *The Folklore of Management*. Boston, Little, Brown and Co., 1961 (New York, New American Library, Mentor Books, 1962, p. 54).

15 Facts about response to income questions in the 1960 census are from *U.S. Census of Population: 1960, General Social and Economic Characteristics, United States Summary*, Table C-2.

17 Senator Charles Tobey's radio address on February 19, 1940, is quoted in *Hearings Before a Subcommittee of the Committee on Commerce on S. Res. 231*, 76th Congress, 3rd Session, February, 1940, p. 63.

17 Representative Clarence Brown's charge was quoted in *The New York Times*, December 7, 1949.

28 Robert L. Heilbroner, *The Future as History*. New York, Harper & Row, Publishers, 1960 (New York, Grove Press, Evergreen Books, 1961, p. 119).

30 The 1930 figures for farms without electricity are from U.S. Bureau of the Census, *Historical Statistics of the United States, Colonial Times to 1957*, Series S 70–80.

30 The 1940 figures for homes without inside toilets are from *U. S. Census of Housing: 1940, Vol. II, General Characteristics*, Table 6B.

30 President Roosevelt's statement is quoted in Sumner H. Slichter, *Economic Growth in the United States*. Baton Rouge, La., Louisiana State University Press, 1961 (New

York, The Crowell-Collier Publishing Co., Collier Books, 1963, p. 19).

31 Gabriel Kolko, *Wealth and Power in America*. New York, Frederick A. Praeger, Inc., 1962, Preface and p. 129.

32 Figures on the use of hamburger and steak at different income levels are from U.S. Department of Agriculture, *Food Consumption of Households in the United States*, Household Food Consumption Survey, 1955, Report No. 1, pp. 66–67.

32 Kolko, *op. cit.*, p. 13.

34 Facts showing that incomes were more equally distributed in the period after World War II than in 1929 when allowance is made for undistributed profits are from Selma Goldsmith, and others, "Size Distribution of Income Since the Mid-Thirties," *Review of Economics and Statistics*, February, 1954, p. 20.

34 Facts showing income distribution including capital gains and losses are from M. Liebenberg and J. M. Fitzwilliams, "Size Distribution of Personal Income, 1957–60," *Survey of Current Business*, May 1961, p. 14.

36 Tax figures on lines 6–8 from bottom are from U.S. Bureau of the Census, *Statistical Abstract of the United States: 1962*, p. 415.

37 Arthur F. Burns, *Looking Forward*, 31st Annual Report of the National Bureau of Economic Research, p. 4.

37 Paul A. Samuelson, *Economics: An Introductory Analysis*, 5th ed. New York, McGraw-Hill Book Co., Inc., 1961, p. 114.

37 Editors of *Fortune*, *The Changing American Market*. New York, Garden City Books (Hanover House), 1955, p. 52.

38 Sumner H. Slichter, *Economic Growth in the United States*. Baton Rouge, La., Louisiana State University Press, 1961 (New York, The Crowell-Collier Publishing Co., Collier Books, 1963, pp. 29–30).

38 Arnold J. Toynbee, *Civilization on Trial*. New York, Oxford University Press, 1948, p. 25.

38 Thorstein Veblen, *The Theory of the Leisure Class.* New York, The Modern Library, 1934, pp. 102–114.

40 Joseph A. Kahl, *The American Class Structure.* New York, Holt, Rinehart and Winston, Inc., 1957, p. 99.

44, 46 Department of Labor figures used to compare earnings of skilled and unskilled factory workers are from Harry Ober, "Occupational Wage Differentials, 1907–1947," *Monthly Labor Review*, August, 1948.

52 Pareto's Law has been widely discussed in economic literature. Excellent summaries may be found in *Income in the United States—Its Amount and Distribution*, Vol. 2. New York, National Bureau of Economic Research, 1922. Also in A. C. Pigou, *Economics of Welfare*, 3rd ed. London, Macmillan and Co., 1929, Part 4, Chap. 2.

54 Michael Quill's statement was quoted in the Washington *Post*, January 28, 1963.

54 William O. Douglas, *Freedom of the Mind.* New York, American Library Association in cooperation with the Public Affairs Committee, Inc., Public Affairs Pamphlet No. 3, 1962, p. 2.

56 Leon H. Keyserling, *Poverty and Deprivation in the U.S.* Washington, D.C., Conference on Economic Progress, April, 1962.

56 Charles Booth, *Life and Labour of the People in London,* 2nd ed. London and Edinburgh, Williams and Norgate, 1889.

57 Statement that one-third of the people in American cities have "insufficient incomes" was made by Dorothy S. Brady, *Hearings before the Subcommittee on Low-Income Families*, Joint Committee on the Economic Report, 81st Congress, 1st Session, 1949, p. 475.

58 Facts cited for Harlan County are from *U.S. Census of Housing: 1960, Vol. I, States and Small Areas*, Table 30.

59 The report concluding that in 1957 the lowest fifth of families were in low-income status is from Robert J. Lampman, *The Low-Income Population and Economic Growth*, Study Paper No. 12, Joint Economic Committee, 86th Congress, 1st Session, 1959, p. 4.

59 Facts about the Bacons are from *Making Ends Meet on Less Than $2,000 a Year*, Joint Committee on the Economic Report, 82nd Congress, 1st Session, 1951, p. 126.

70 The *Harper's* quotation is from John Fischer, "The Stupidity Problem," *Harper's Magazine*, September 1962.

71 Michael Harrington, *The Other America*. New York, The Macmillan Co., 1962, p. 45.

71 Facts about the Wood case are from *Making Ends Meet on Less Than $2,000 a Year, op. cit.*, p. 37.

75 Facts about the Scilaro family are from the above source, p. 84.

77 The study showing economic loss caused by racial discrimination was made by the Council of Economic Advisers, *Statement of Economic Costs of Racial Discrimination*, September, 1962.

79 Facts about the Duncans, Mahoneys, and Petrovs are from *Making Ends Meet on Less Than $2,000 a Year, op. cit.*, pp. 31, 32, 98.

81 Dorothy S. Brady, "Research on Size Distribution of Income," *Studies in Income and Wealth*, Vol. 13. New York, National Bureau of Economic Research, 1951, p. 30.

82 The Bureau of Labor Statistics estimate of the cost of a "modest but adequate" level of living is from Helen H. Lamale and Margaret S. Stotz, "The Interim City Worker's Family Budget," *Monthly Labor Review*, August, 1960, Table 3; and U.S. Department of Labor, *Workers' Budgets in the United States*, Bulletin No. 927.

83 President Roosevelt's statement is quoted in *Inaugural Addresses of the Presidents of the United States*, House Document No. 540, 82nd Congress, 2nd Session, 1952, p. 231.

84 President Kennedy's nationwide address was quoted in the Washington *Post*, June 12, 1963.

97–98 Jacob K. Javits, *Discrimination U.S.A.* New York, Washington Square Press, 1962, p. 88.

98 U.S. Department of Labor, *The Economic Situation of Negroes in the United States*, Bulletin S-3, revised, 1962, p. 6.

102–103 Quincy Mumford's speech was quoted in the Washington *Post*, July 5, 1963.

105 The Department of Labor estimate of the income needed in 1959 by a family of four living in New York City is from Helen H. Lamale and Margaret S. Stotz, "The Interim City Worker's Family Budget," *Monthly Labor Review*, August, 1960, Table 3.

108 Figures quoted for rents paid by Puerto Ricans in New York City are from *U.S. Census of Housing: 1960, Metropolitan Housing*, Table A-16.

110 The argument that the average Puerto Rican would rather live in Puerto Rico than New York is from A. J. Jaffe, ed., "Demographic and Labor Force Characteristics of the New York City Puerto Rican Population," *Puerto Rican Population of New York City*, a series of papers delivered before the New York area chapter of the American Statistical Association, October 21, 1953; New York, Columbia University, Bureau of Applied Social Research, January, 1954, p. 24.

110 Christopher Rand, *The Puerto Ricans*. New York, Oxford University Press, 1958, p. 52.

111–112 *Ibid.*, p. 44.

114 The figures in the section on Spanish-Americans are for those who are white. The comparison throughout, therefore, is between white Spanish-Americans and other whites.

118 The statement by Lyle Saunders is quoted in Carey McWilliams, *Brothers Under the Skin*. Boston, Little, Brown and Company, 1951, p. 131.

120 The quotation from the Meriam Report is from the above source, p. 79.

121 Will Herberg, *Protestant-Catholic-Jew*. New York, Doubleday & Company, Inc., 1955 (Anchor Books, 1960, p. 9).

125 President Kennedy's statement is from *Economic Report of the President*, January, 1962, pp. 9–10.

126 Paul A. Samuelson, *Economics: An Introductory Analy-*

sis, 5th ed. New York, McGraw-Hill Book Co., Inc., 1961, p. 111.

127 Facts about sources of income for the top five percent of the families are from U.S. Bureau of the Census, *Current Population Reports—Consumer Income,* Series P-60, No. 37, Table 15.

128 Figures for the top one percent of the families living on unearned income are from unpublished data of the Bureau of the Census.

128 Figures for working wives in the top income group are from U.S. Bureau of the Census, *Current Population Reports—Consumer Income,* Series P-60, No. 37, Table 3.

128 Figures for the families in the top five percent with three or more workers are from the above source, Table 7.

132 Morris R. Cohen, *American Thought.* New York, The Free Press of Glencoe, 1954 (New York, The Crowell-Collier Publishing Co., Collier Books, 1962, p. 48).

133 The editors of *Fortune* are quoted in Frederick Lewis Allen, *The Big Change.* New York, Harper & Row, Publishers, 1952 (New York, Bantam Books, Inc., 1961, p. 215).

133 Frederick Lewis Allen's Statement is from the above source, p. 216.

140 Christopher Rand, *The Puerto Ricans.* New York, Oxford University Press, 1958, p. 73.

140 James Baldwin, *Nobody Knows My Name.* New York, The Dial Press, Inc., 1961 (New York, Dell Publishing Co., Inc., 1962, p. 106).

142 Seymour E. Harris, *The Market for College Graduates and Related Aspects of Education and Income.* Cambridge, Mass., Harvard University Press, 1949, p. 64.

142 Opinions expressed by James B. Conant and William J. Wallin can be found in C. Wright Mills, *White Collar.* New York, Oxford University Press (Galaxy Books), 1951, p. 270.

146 Quotations about apprenticeship programs are from

Harry Kursh, *Apprenticeships in America*. New York, W. W. Norton & Company, Inc., 1958, p. 65.

157 Eli Ginzberg, *The Negro Potential*. New York, Columbia University Press, 1956, pp. 58, 53.

160–161 The 1962 figures for Negroes employed in federal jobs are from House of Representatives, 88th Congress, 1st Session, Document No. 75, *Message from the President of the United States Relative to Civil Rights*, February 28, 1963, pp. 8–9.

162 The 1960 income figures for families with college students are from unpublished data used in U.S. Bureau of the Census, *Current Population Reports—Population Characteristics*, Series P-20, No. 110, Table 10.

162 Figures for college students whose fathers were not college graduates are from the above source.

162 The 1959 figures for the sources of financial support of college students are from U.S. Bureau of the Census, *Educational Status, College Plans, and Occupational Status of Farm and Nonfarm Youths: October 1959*, Series P-27, No. 30, Table A.

162–163 The 1959 figures for high school seniors planning to go to college are from Maxine G. Stewart, "Who Goes to College?" *Occupational Outlook Quarterly*, May 1962, p. 12.

165 Facts about the relation between performance ability and college attendance are from Charles B. Nam and James C. Cowhig, "Ability and College Attendance," *Occupational Outlook Quarterly*, December, 1962, p. 34.

166 James N. Morgan, and others, *Income and Welfare in the United States*. New York, McGraw-Hill Book Co., Inc., 1962, p. 51.

168 The figures of the Bureau of Labor Statistics for budget costs in New York, Los Angeles, and Chicago are from Helen H. Lamale and Margaret S. Stotz, "The Interim City Worker's Family Budget," *Monthly Labor Review*, August, 1960, Table 3.

168 Unofficial figures for physicians' earnings are from articles reprinted in *Physicians' Earnings and Expenses*.

Oradell, New Jersey, Medical Economics, Inc., 1961, pp. 6, 10.

169 Unofficial figures for chemical engineers' earnings are from David A. H. Roethel, *1960 Chemical Salaries*. Washington, D.C., American Chemical Society, 1961, p. 119.

189-190 Facts about supplementary earners are from Jacob Schiffman, "Marital and Family Characteristics of Workers, March 1961," *Monthly Labor Review*, January, 1962, Table 4.

190-191 Frederick Lewis Allen, *Only Yesterday*. New York, Harper & Row, Publishers, 1931 (New York, Bantam Books, Inc., 1959, p. 68).

193 Michael Harrington, *The Other America*. New York, The Macmillan Co., 1962, p. 179.

196 Facts about husbands who were asked what they thought about working wives are from James N. Morgan, and others, *op. cit.*, p. 112.

197 Katherine B. Oettinger, "Maternal Employment and Children," *Work in the Lives of Married Women* (National Manpower Council). New York, Columbia University Press, 1958, p. 143.

198 Facts about young mothers whose husbands earned more than $7,000 in 1961 are from Jacob Schiffman, "Marital and Family Characteristics of Workers, March 1961," *Monthly Labor Review*, January, 1962, Table M.

198 Facts about mothers of children under age three in 1959 are from Jacob Schiffman, "Family Characteristics of Workers: 1959," *Monthly Labor Review*, August, 1960, Table F.

198 Facts about the care of children of working mothers are from James N. Morgan, and others, *op. cit.*, p. 111.

198-199 Figures for the types of jobs held by working wives are from Jacob Schiffman, "Marital and Family Characteristics of Workers, March 1961," *Monthly Labor Review*, January, 1962, Table 5.

199 Figures for the earnings of working wives are from the above source, p. 12.

200 Constantius' law was quoted in John Hajnal, "The Pros-

pects for Population Forecasts," *Journal of the American Statistical Association*, June, 1955, p. 309.

200 The estimate of 75 million families and unrelated individuals in 1980 is derived from U.S. Bureau of the Census, *Statistical Abstract of the United States, 1962*, p. 42. This estimate assumes one-quarter of the annual change in family formation from 1950 to 1956–58 for the period 1957 to 1965. It was assumed that there would be no change thereafter. The published census estimates are 60,980,000 families and 9,888,000 primary unrelated individuals. It was assumed that there would be 4,000,000 secondary unrelated individuals in 1980.

201 The estimate of about 2.5 percent increase in family income each year is from National Planning Association, *Regional Projections to 1976*, Technical Supplement No. 8, February, 1962, p. 65.

201 Sidney G. Tickton, *Letter to a College President*, New York, Fund for the Advancement of Education, May 1963, p. 23.

204 The estimate of the percentage of young people who will attend college in 1980 is from the above source, p. 19.

204 Facts about the changing composition of the labor force are from U.S. Department of Labor, *Manpower: Challenge of the 1960's*, p. 11.

207–208 W. H. Ferry, *Caught on the Horn of Plenty*. New York, Bulletin of the Center for the Study of Democratic Institutions, January, 1962, p. 3.

208 W. Allen Wallis' statement is from *Automation and Technological Change*, ed. by John T. Dunlop. Englewood Cliffs, New Jersey, Prentice-Hall, Inc., 1962, pp. 110–111.

208 John W. Kendrick's statement was quoted in the Washington *Post*, May 18, 1963.

208 Figures for output and man hours between 1947 and 1961 are from U.S. Department of Labor, *Manpower Report of the President*, March, 1963, p. 4.

210–212 Statement by Under Secretary of Labor John F. Henning before the Senate Committee on Labor and Public Welfare, June 4, 1963.

212–213 The prediction that, by 1975, 85 percent of all Negroes will live in northern cities is from Dan Morgan, "The Wesleyan Tutorials," *Saturday Review*, June 15, 1963, p. 69.

214 Figures on Negro and white children in fatherless homes are from *U.S. Census of Population: 1960, Detailed Characteristics, United States Summary*, Table 185.

216 The appraisal of the 1940 census data is from Edwin D. Goldfield, "Decennial Census and Current Population Survey Data on Income," *Studies in Income and Wealth*, Vol. 23. Princeton, N.J., Princeton University Press, 1958, p. 43. This volume was based on a conference sponsored by the National Bureau of Economic Research.

217 The quotation explaining why income questions were changed to 20 percent coverage is from the above source, p. 56.

218 Facts about nonrespondents in the 1950 census are from the above source, pp. 211–212.

220 International Labor Office, *Family Living Studies*. Geeva, Switzerland, 1961, pp. 221–244.

Index